DOWN-BACK

PERSONAL ESSAYS AND POETIC THOUGHTS
FROM A GOOD OLE BOY

Terry Lovelette

Chapin Keith Publishing
Daleville, VA. 24083
www.chapinkeith.com

Publisher's Cataloging-in-Publication Data

Names: Lovelette, Terry - author.
Title: DOWN-BACK / Terry Lovelette.

Identifiers: LCCN 2024923144 (print) | ISBN 979-8-9919038-1-3 (hardcover) | ISBN 979-8-9919038-0-6 (paperback) | ISBN 979-8-9919038-2-0 (eBook).

Subjects: LCSH: American poetry--Male authors. | Men--Biography. | Outdoor recreation--Psychological aspects--Biography. | Poetry. | BISAC: POETRY / American / General. | BIOGRAPHY & AUTOBIOGRAPHY / Memoirs.

Classification: LCC PS3612.O99 D98 2024 (print) | LCC PS3612.O99 (ebook) | DDC 811/.6--dc23.

Cover and book design by Asya Blue Design.

Cover photo by Sherry King.
All other photos by are by Terry Lovelette except as noted.

First Edition

This book is dedicated to the countless voices of wisdom that have graced my path. You taught me to seek, and to find, the reliable beauty and meaningful goodness in life. Thank you for your guidance and your love! To all my childhood friends and the memories of our adventures "Down Back." In special remembrance of three good friends who left this life too soon. Brucey, Jeff, and Little Jamie–your spirits live on.

Praise for DOWN-BACK

"Terry Lovelette has an inquiring mind and a pilgrim's heart. With this book, he takes the reader along on some of his pilgrimages, many involving hikes in the mountains that have given him uncommon insight into what it means to live fully and well. His wanderings and wonderings have taken him far and wide—but because he travels with open eyes and an open heart, he always returns to a place called home, a place where life can be seen steadily and whole. We live in disorienting times, surrounded by voices saying that up is down and wrong is right. May the essays, poems and photos in this beautiful little book help you as they have helped me reclaim a sense of true north."

—Parker J. Palmer (author of *A Hidden Wholeness*, *Let Your Life Speak*, and *Healing the Heart of Democracy*)

Contents

Preface

A few years ago, my daughter (Molly) and I started to get together once a month for lunch. It provided us with a chance to catch-up with each other in a relaxed setting while allowing conversation to flow in a manner befitting an adult daughter and her father. Over the course of time, we covered various topics as we got to know each other a little bit more in the current stages of our lives. A very rewarding experience in and of itself. In one of our discussions, she asked me about what things I like to do, or what hobbies I engaged in that I enjoyed that she wasn't aware of. As it was, I mentioned that I liked to write. Blessed with a curious mind, she probed and asked questions. In the process of our discussion, I explained that I like to write poetry and reflective essays to help me sort out my thoughts. I also mentioned that I secretly thought about writing a book. I recall telling Molly that I already had the title of my book picked out. It would be called *"DOWN-BACK"* in honor of my childhood friends and in reverence of the special nature of the woods that we played in behind our houses on High Street in Sheldon Springs, VT. I told her about the deep meaning that this location had for me and also expressed how grateful I was for having the good fortune to grow up the way that I did and with the people that I was surrounded by. When she asked me when I might write this book, I had no answer. In fact, I remember driving home from lunch with words of self-doubt ringing in my ears. You know, the usual stuff. Things like who are you to write a book? What do you have to say that's special and who cares what you think? Truth be known; I still wonder about that.

But as fate would have it, my daughter took the proverbial bull-by-the-horns and forced my hand. For Father's Day, 2019, she gave me a StoryWorth account as a gift. With this account, I would be asked a series of weekly questions throughout the next year. My mission, if you will, was to ponder the question each week and then write a reflection. As I did, my responses were catalogued within my account. At the end of the year (July of 2020) my responses were pulled together, printed, and bound into a book that was shared with family and close friends. That effort also laid the groundwork for the publication of this book and that's how it came to be.

The Tarn

O verall, I have had a blessed life and have an abundance of things to be grateful for. In general, my definition of happiness has evolved as I have aged and become more aware of my spiritual self. I don't pretend to have anything perfected with regard to my spiritual self, but that awareness has changed the many perceptions that I was attached to. Being willing to let go of societies definition of happiness has been a good practice. In my opinion, that definition is rooted in the outcome of externally driven events from people, places, and things. The lasting effect of externally driven happiness is fleeting. Joy on the other hand, is a better definition for me. Again, it's just what I have come to believe, but joy is more consistent and cultivated within me at the soul level. It comes when you make peace with who you are, why you are, and how you are. The result of such joy is that it develops into a heart filled with gratitude. A grateful heart pumps grace throughout your body and feeds the mind with thoughts that are based in the root of universal love. In my opinion, elements of that love consist of compassion, patience, understanding, tolerance, kindness, forgiveness, acceptance, empathy, and mutual respect. Frankly the list of words and actions to describe the essence of this perennial philosophy are lengthy. I define them all as love and I define love as God's grace.

How one connects with love is a personal choice. My choice is to take regular journeys into nature. Not everyone understands my choice or my connection and that's OK to me. To each their own; I respect that each person gets to have their own opinion and make their own choice. As for me, I know the action that I need to take and that action is to go into nature. When I do, I often experience moments that leave me with a deep feeling of reverence. Sometimes these experiences are ephemeral where the universe presents breathtaking beauty and profound moments to me. When these experiences occur, I struggle to catch up with what just happened. I can't explain these moments, but I can increase the likelihood of experiencing them by simply being outside and into nature. One such moment occurred at a magnificent location in the Sierra Nevada in the early morning hours. A poem of that experience follows and a picture of the location is below.

The Tarn just south of Pinchot Pass Sierra Nevada Mountains CA

The Tarn

stillness of the morning the tarn is calm
reflective images from the light of dawn
somewhere a struggle of selfish thought
here at the tarn a struggle not

serene the moment as I stand in awe
the world afar so full of flaw
deep in my soul an ember sparks
ephemeral peace the ridge line stark

a fleeting joy or a lasting place
memories made loves embrace
greater thoughts flood my brain
a simple human I resist and refrain

small speck of dust in the cosmic flow
challenging the grasp of the universal glow
what will it be as I leave from here
a joyous heart or a mind of fear

the clever muse within me plays
my gracious deity have your way
soak up the essence of the grateful morn
with warmth inside a faith reborn

accept the path as it comes my way
thy will not mine the mystery each day
my trek goes on my journey too
the tarn it seems provides a clue

If I attempted to explain the feeling of joy that was my experience at "The Tarn" I would miss the mark by a wide margin. I simply sum it up as God's grace. Without that grace I am in a constant search to fill a void in my soul. I have been in that abyss, felt the emptiness, and experienced the anguish. I do not care to return there. With that grace, I am fulfilled. There is little that I need and nothing to search for. The inner peace provided by this universal love is compelling. Each day I surrender to grace a little more. As I do, I make progress and I continue to wake up. My awareness increases and my potential to experience joy grows. This joy enables me to embrace life with love and it fills my heart with gratitude.

Poetry and Place

Some time ago, at a *Thoughts from a Walk* book signing event, I listened to feedback about poetry. Like the world we live in, opinions varied but each one offered came from another's point of view. Frankly, a perspective that I can never have. Simply because I will never be another person. Yet, if I remain open, my mind expands when I consider the input from someone else. I don't have to agree with it and my own perspective doesn't have to be more correct than another point of view. I just need to consider their viewpoint as part of the interconnected flow of life that I share with everyone else.

For me, poetry helps that "flow of life process" move along. The poet has to engage his will to allow the process to start. Then move his body to create the motion of thought. This action awakens the mind as sweat beads on your forehead and rivers down your face. Somehow time slows in this environment, and a pathway to the heart is opened. Petty grievances fall away and the spirit of the day unfolds in front of you. Beautiful examples of life that persists. You have no choice but to look at them with deep appreciation. Each example is holy and that holiness fills the soul. Then, you jot down a few thoughts. Someone else might read those thoughts and find some connection. That connection restarts the process and increases the flow. In its own time and in its own way. Just like nature.

Every day nature holds an abundance of moments like this. In society though, quite often the moments come at you from "out in left field" and in a loud voice. Awkward even, as you backpedal a bit trying to discern where another's rant is coming from. Most of the time, I have no idea. Thus, I don't take it personally. Instead, I soldier on trying to do my best at being better while I make my way within the human condition.

I have discovered that I make my way better when I slow it all down and take a walk in the woods. Close encounters with creatures enlarge you. Making eye contact with an animal in the wild touches you in that inner place where it all stirs. A reservoir of our deepest emotions held in pools filled with Angst and Grace. The one you drink from dictates how you will be. Anxious and edgy or peaceful and serene. Your choice.

With inspiration from Rick Kempa *Truths of the Trail* (1), I'm reminded to consider how I move through life. Mindlessly chugging away or walking within the spirit of Grace and gratitude? When I'm open to the spirit of Grace, it's easier to remember that every step that I take is fueled by the gift of breath. That simple reflex action of life is a treasure to appreciate. To me it doesn't matter what anyone else decides to call the donor of this precious gift or if there even is anyone to thank. Opinions vary and theories abound. What's pertinent here is the choice that I get to make. In other words, which reservoir do I drink from? The one filled with Grace or the one filled with Angst? That choice will determine what it is that rises from within, it can be a source of agitation and discontent, forces of isolation that separate you onto an island of loneliness. Or, it can be a source of well-being that sates you and connects you with the flow of life. A place of restful solitude where it's okay to be okay.

Each morning, after I take care of the daily rituals of life, I get to stand on the ground and appreciate where my feet are connected. I make a point of visiting nature on a regular basis. With my hiking boots laced up I move along. Breathing in the day, feeling the elements on my skin, smelling the aromas of the landscape, and soaking in the visions of this place. All of this welcomes me in as a guest. It is my good fortune that I get to be here. Try as I might, I do leave a trace. Footprints in the mud that I trod upon appear. Wherever it is that I go, I make an impact and the location is different because of my presence. It stays that way for some time after I leave. Eventually, rain washes in and my tracks get absorbed into the mud. Sometimes, other elements like leaves or fallen branches coverup the boot prints that I make. I wish that I could say that I leave something better with nature. But frankly, the best that I can seem to do is to offer my deepest respect. Yet, in nature's unselfish spirit of reciprocity, blessings are offered to me and I am different too in a more positive manner. Because of the place I have the good fortune of walking in, I get to experience its offerings. Little treasures in their natural settings presented as gifts of life.

All of the places that I've walked are stored inside of me. Held within the reservoir of emotions that exist in my own vessel of life. These blessed places openly share their Grace and offer a more perfect peace. I want to believe that my walking life will continue with no end. The way the trails do before me and behind me. But I accept that this is not the case. Someday, it will end. Until that time, I'll keep moving along. Appreciating these little moments in time and letting the poetry of life fill my reservoir of emotions with Grace. We live in a beautiful place and I'm grateful that I have another day. In the calamity of our times, saying Yes to life, makes all the difference. In my humble opinion, there is beautiful poetry in that choice. Be well and all the best!

What is Poetry

In a world full of wonder
Learn things anew
It will never fail you
Always true

A walk in the forest
Springtime fresh
Sunshine and shadows
Yugen bliss

Drop the misery
Of cruel fearful men
Swindlers and scoundrels
Selfish within

Instead reap the joy
From the wisdom of yore
Seek courage to journey
Our heartstrings implore

Flowers break through
A long winters rest
Colorful glory
Serenity's best

Ghost like visions
Float through the trees
White flags flashing
Darting with ease

Never exhausted
This beauty of place
Natures abundance
The essence of Grace

Eagle Mountain, Milton, VT

Mentors of the Mountains

In the 80's, when I was in my 20's, I had the good fortune of spending time with two experienced backcountry men. They were 20-30 years older than me. They were both extreme outdoorsmen with extensive mountain resumes. They were also humble and kind.

At the time, Pat and Ralph were doing things that I was dreaming about. Long distance hiking, climbing mountains, and engaging in backcountry adventures. In today's world of social media, they would be labeled as "badass" adventure enthusiasts. To make it even more special, Ralph was a type 1 diabetic and a Black American. A true trail blazer who was full of resilience and inspiration. Neither Pat nor Ralph was cocky or egocentric. Instead, they both came across with quiet confidence and a deep respect for the mountains.

Spending time with them was like going to school. Both of these gentlemen exuded a wisdom about the mountains that only comes with time and the reality of facing yourself in challenging situations. Thus, they faced the mountains with respect, rigorous honesty, and humility.

Of the many lessons that they willingly passed on to me, a few stand out as sage advice. We had extensive conversations about the necessity of leaving your ego at the trailhead and discussions about what that meant. They schooled me on the importance of the ten essentials. About the necessity of conducting research in preparation of the trail or area that you will be adventuring in. Of having an itinerary, sticking to it and leaving it with someone at home. They explained the truth about the difficulties of assessing challenges, knowing when to bail, and how to be mentally strong enough to make those decisions. They drilled me on the importance of establishing a turnaround time, how to calculate it, why you needed to have one, and the absolute truth about not letting my ego overpower risk assessment and logical reasoning. They recalled occurrences when injury, the need for help from search and rescue, even death, resulted from poor decision making by folks that they knew. Somber realities to remember and respect.

In the mountains, there is the harsh reality of one's own personal limits. If you push those limits too far, then you might reach the point of no return. To be clear, YOU could die. Thanks to Pat and Ralph, I learned that it is imperative to understand that there is no shame in managing your own safety and survival. There is no embarrassment in erring on the side of caution. There is no failure in turning around and leaving the mountain for another day. In fact, it's my responsibility to respect these truths. Over the years I have faced various backcountry challenges and difficult situations. But, as the result of the solid mentoring from Pat and Ralph, I have no harrowing experiences to retell.

I seek adventure to challenge myself, to get uncomfortable, and to experience the elements as they are. Firsthand, raw, and real. In doing that I push my own limits. I've had the good fortune of accumulating experience in Alaska, the Canadian Rockies, Northeastern Quebec, the Sierra Nevada, Yellowstone, the Tetons, Colorado, Utah, Arizona, and throughout the Northeast. In the last decade and a half, routinely hiking over 1000 miles each year, many times alone. In all of these adventures, I have walked with a healthy respect for the mountains. If I have doubts about the time of day, my own abilities, those of a hiking partner, or the conditions on the mountain, I accept the truth of the situation and either setup shelter or turn around. Whatever the circumstances call for and depending on the type of outing that I'm on (day hike, multi day, etc.). A good hike is a safe hike. The summit will be there for another day. Thank you Pat and Ralph for drilling these truths into my head.

Jasper National Park, Alberta, Canada

Reflections from Wheeler Pond

O n one occasion, Sherry and I spent some time at the Hadsel/Mares camp at Wheeler Pond to celebrate the completion of my 62nd trip around the sun. (Thanks, GMC, for this peaceful place.)

In the bigger picture, this was an event that has significance in being insignificant. Taken individually, we are all just a speck of dust in the cosmic flow. Living on a planet that has been floating around in space for roughly a few billion years, all of us here on earth exist for just a brief moment in time, yet (I believe) we all come with a purpose, even people that we might not agree with. An important distinction to make amidst the chaos and confusion of the daily grind. (I'll get to that point in a minute.)

Sometimes, the grind can seem rather pointless to me as I sit on the sidelines and watch the back-and-forth banter ensue between those drawn by the pull of political division. The constant drone echoing through the airwaves gets rather stale for my taste and the grind of dualism in our society can simply wear a person down. It rings true to my ears that the vortex of the EGO is a powerful force that can suck anyone into the abyss, I believe that the din and clamor created by that force can tire the soul. With just a sliver of awareness, hope remains within the spirit.

I need to be reminded every now and again that I should not yield to the weariness of the spirit. That the world's cares and distractions will intrude and make me weak. It's up to me, in times like this, to carry on and take the required steps to renew my spirit so that it will become strong again. Believe as you will, but it's my belief that God's spirit is always with me, however I can silence that grace if I give-in to the relentless pull of the EGO's force. When I give-in, my soul gets weary. This weariness can come at me in various ways but it always leaves me anxious and with a feeling that's physically and mentally exhausting. When I'm in that state of life, it's incumbent upon me to do something about it. If not, then I can get sucked into the worldly grind just like anybody else.

Over the course of time, the threads of dualistic and egocentric thinking have become tightly woven into all of us. Awareness of that reality helps a person remain cognizant of the negative side effects that come with a dualistic mindset. Unfortunately for me (and perhaps all of us), is that the first clue that I'm slipping into that mindset is when others start to irritate me more. It's a spiritual axiom of sorts that helps me understand that my lack of acceptance, and the inner conflict that comes with it, is resolved by a change in my attitude toward the person, place, or thing that I hold in contempt. The truth then, is that the solution rests within me and a change in my attitude provides the remedy. The EGO, on the other hand, flips it around on us and gets us thinking that others are the ones in need of changing. Coming to the realization that the responsibility for my inner peace rests with me isn't always welcomed news. That realization forces me to surrender to a Higher Power that can provide the needed courage to see that a shift of consciousness has occurred within me and that adjustments need to be made in my attitude. In my case, this practice is a process and not an event. Faith helps and it creates a pathway that leads me to a vista where my line of sight is unobstructed. It takes energy to get to that place and oftentimes I simply trudge along. But a slow and steady effort leads me to a spot where I can rise above the fog, get to a place of quiet, gain an element of equilibrium in my attitude and outlook on life, and wait for the power of the spirit to flow back in. I'm grateful for this awareness (and on a good day) blessed with that grace, it settles my unrest.

Nature provides an entryway for me that opens a door to a place where I can connect to a greater purpose. That connection, then, allows me to find a significance in my insignificance and a purposeful meaning to my existence. I don't mean to imply that I have anything perfected in life. That truth should be somewhat self-evident if you read between the lines.

Each of us though, have weathered many storms in life. Like a mountain, we have been chiseled by the forces of nature and come with our own unique character. We also come with a deeper meaning and a deeper purpose that can be realized when we pause and reflect upon our interconnectedness. When we take the time to journey into that uncharted territory, walls of division come down and we can start to reflect on the vulnerable nature of each individual. All of us have elements of vulnerability within us. These elements are reflected back to us from others who hold a similar set of traits. We, in turn, reflect a similar set of traits back to them. If we look between the lily pads of life, we start to see the definition in the reflections and the inner beauty that rests within each other and the common connections that we all share.

As I transition toward the coming year and my next trip around the sun. I hope that these words can bring you some inspiration and serve to help you find some courage to open up the eyes of your own soul. In the reflections, there is a place of brilliance that exists within each of us and it beams a gracious light.

Wheeler Pond

Be still and rest in the silence
Reflections form in quiet waters
A depth of meaning is seen when we look into the moments
The lily pads on the surface form an entryway

With a slightly different perspective
One can embrace the beauty inside of Wheeler Pond
With a bit of courage
We can carry that grace forward upon our departure

Walking with a sense of reverence in our daily journey
Is sure to enable a gait fed by a heart of compassion
And a soul bathed in kindness
Maybe, with a mixture of hope, an essence of empathy comes
with us

When we step away from the busyness of life
It is easier to appreciate that there is a oneness to our existence
And, that it is too often forgotten
Each of us comes from the same place

And, won the race of millions at the moment of our creation
Surely, we can recognize our purpose
And see that an interconnectedness exists in us all
Where the marrow meets the bone

In every walk of life
Lead the way with

Compassion, patience, understanding, tolerance, kindness, respect, and love
Be the good that the world so desperately needs

Wheeler Pond and Wheeler Mountain VT

Lessons of Clarity

On one particular weekend, I had the good fortune of tagging two more 4,000-foot peaks in the White Mountains. Like all of these pursuits, the requisite planning played itself out. Coordination with hiking partners on the route that we would follow, where we would meet, timing, insight on trail knowledge, gear needs, and various other necessities were "kicked around." Perhaps a tedious process for some, but one part of the hiking process that I enjoy. I also find it important to establish a base of open communication among your hiking partners. Over the course of time, this baseline dialogue of honest, respectful, and open communication lessens the chances of unfortunate incidents occurring. This process also affords each person the opportunity to gradually place the desires of their ego on the back-burner. My experience has led me to an understanding that my enjoyment is increased when I leave as much of my ego as possible at the trailhead.

Our goal this weekend was to summit two 4Ker's, Garfield and Galehead. As one should expect, the experience of reaching a 4K foot peak in the Whites for each one in our hiking group would be different. Nate, would be reaching peaks #38 and #39, I would be tagging #11 and #12, Liam would be touching the top of his 3rd and 4th 4K summits (at 11 yrs old and done in the last 2 weeks a very worthy effort!), and Mike would be hitting the top of his 1st and 2nd 4K foot peaks in the Whites. My respect and admiration to each in our group for your personal achievement!

With that range of experiences, ages, and individual points of views, come 4 different perspectives. Each one of us sees reality through our own set of lenses, if you will, that sets the parameters around the depth of the experience that we perceive. I can't speak for anyone else as that segue leads me down a path of judgement and deep into the realm of the ego self. It also puts me into a mindset that takes away from the self-discovery and enjoyment that comes my way through the efforts of a good climb. At my age (62), I don't have many years left to engage in mountain pursuits. Thus, each time I go, I do my best to absorb the experience and be open to receiving the moments of joy that the universe provides.

Sometimes, these moments come from kind gestures that naturally occur while hiking. Every now and again, ascending trekkers pass descending folks. Without much fanfare, polite actions take place. People smile, exchange kind words, and offer the right of way to each other. Rarely, do I see contention in these moments. With few exceptions, respectful interactions lead the way. Observing how I see these exchanges helps me learn more about myself. To be honest, I don't always wear "rose colored glasses" and sometimes I lapse into judgement. (I'll never reach perfection.) But, even then, I get a chance to learn more about myself. As I walk, there is ample time to sort out the mystery of myself. If I dare enter into the realm of self-discovery, the insight that I gain can be brutally honest. As I am, is how I see the world, and the judgement that I'm placing onto others, is in some way, a judgement of myself. What I do with that insight determines what type of perception guides my experience. My default in these moments of frustration or confusion, is to retreat into silence, and to contemplate my thought process, as well as, my associated actions. Am I somehow disturbed by another human being and projecting my inner toxic thoughts onto them or am I viewing others with acceptance, kindness, and respect. A tough question to ask myself sometimes, made tougher when I realize that I've lapsed into a mode of judgement once again. The only way to a peaceful life is through acceptance and when I find a resistance or conflict present in my thinking it is a sure sign that

I need to accept some more. Not a foolproof approach by any stretch of the imagination, but one that is largely contemplative and productive. The net result of that approach is a release of negative thinking that might be polluting my mental clarity. I don't know how I appear to others when I'm in the midst of this process. Perhaps a little foggy, because oftentimes, that's the mindset that I'm walking around with during these times of quiet contemplation. So be it, I enjoy this process and find it to be a healthy part of my mental well-being.

When I have enough fortitude to walk the trails in a contemplative manner, the universe kindly returns moments to me that heighten my senses and provide opportunities of gratitude to flourish. As that grace allows, I do my best to be open and available to see the beauty as it unfolds. In my human form, that enlightenment isn't always apparent to me when it occurs. This weekend, I was fortunate to be blessed with some of that divine intervention at the summit of Garfield. I'll get to that in a minute. Prior to the summit, we slogged away at the trail and made our way. Most of the hike was pretty straightforward, and in many ways, typical. As a group, we started together and exchanged our spots on the trail as circumstances played themselves out. Sometimes walking as a pack, sometimes in groups of two or three, and sometimes each walking along as an individual but always being held together through our awareness of each other, and through the relentless efforts of "Nali the wonder dog" as she ran back and forth checking on each of us to make sure we were ok. If ever a soul needs an example of what living in the moment with love means, spend some time with Nali. She radiates love.

In our pre-hike discussions, we had agreed to hike down from the Garfield Ridge Trail to the Garfield tent sites first to secure a camping location for the night, set-up our tents, and to dump off our heavy gear in our tents as well. The hike down to the tent sites from the trail junction of Garfield Ridge and Garfield summit was approximately 0.2 miles. While not very long in distance, it was a very rough and sharp descent. Once settled at the campsite, we agreed on a time to head to the summit, which was now approximately 0.4 miles of a very rough and steep ascent. Information gathered in some pre-hike trail research stated that the trail is an old avalanche site with water flowing through it. Which implied that it's not easy. I was not to be disappointed; the climb up was a grind. As we engaged in the ascent over a jumble of rocks, my instincts took over. As a pudgy ole boy, during these types of climbs, I need to go inside of myself and focus on the next step to make sure that I keep a sure and steady pace going. Most of the time, ascents of this nature push me well outside of my comfort zone, leave me sweat soaked, and force my lungs to work near their maximum potential. Working through these climbs tests my inner resolve and requires me to dig a little deeper than I care to in order to reach the top. A process that challenges my physical capabilities and enhances my mental acuity. But it also affords me the opportunity to embrace the humility that comes from facing the immediate challenges that the mountain places in front of me. By the grace of some power greater than me, I get a chance to make my way through the mountain that day.

Experiences of this nature also present a breeding ground for moments of clarity, reverence if you're so inclined, toward nature's power and beauty that is only seen from the summit. We can also experience a mutual respect of sorts for other hikers who trudged the same path to get there. When in this mind-space, it reminds me that we all have to pay a price to get to the top of anything and that we all have to overcome inner challenges to get there. As I stepped up to the summit of Mt. Garfield, I first took a couple of minutes to allow my breathing to regain its normal cadence. I wiped the sweat from my brow, and let the warm summer breeze flow through my quick dry shirt (which was completely soaked with sweat). In parallel, my eyes and mind raced around trying to take in the views. On this particular evening, and in this particular setting, they were magnificent. Soon a quiet appreciation started to make its way into my thought process. As it did, my desire to capture the best image of the beauty in front of me subsided. In its place came a thought to embrace the stillness and observe. Looking around I could see a couple together on a remote rock outcropping and sharing a bite to eat. That image reminded me of the many times I have done that with Sherry and the mutual joy that comes in those moments. There were a few others who had staked out similar locations and they too appeared to be soaking in the moments. I saw a guy full of excitement, jumping from rock to rock like a flash and in a comical way, seemingly looking for the absolute best spot to sit down and take it all in. There were 3 photographers conversing about the best spot to set-up the cameras for their evening shoot. There were a few others enjoying their time as well. Then there was my hiking group. Nate on 4K summit #38, Liam on 4K summit #4, and Mike standing at the top of his 1st. Each one of them with their own perspective but with smiles on their faces. Of course, Nali was there too. I'm not sure what she was thinking, but I'm quite certain she was smiling too.

Within these moments there was one that left me with a deep feeling of profundity with regard to the definition of love. Amidst all the folks milling around at the summit (a dozen or so) there was an 11-year-old boy and his dad sharing serene moments together as they emanated an aura of love. The two of them were completely enraptured in capturing the mountain experience and sharing words that reflected their joy. To anyone within earshot, it was a gift from the universe that brought with it a perfect example of what love is. With all the chaos and confusion that takes place in the day-to-day grind in society, there are moments of grace available for all of us to witness if we just rub the sleep from our eyes and wake-up ever so slightly. I feel fortunate to have been touched by that grace at the top of Mt. Garfield. It was the highpoint of my weekend and I'm grateful to have been present enough to witness their connection. Of all the views that I was able to see this weekend (and there were plenty) this moment I just described was far and away the best one. In the words of Alfred Wainwright (2): "The precious moments of life are too rare, too valuable to be forgotten when they have passed; we should hoard them as a miser hoards his gold, and bring them to light and rejoice over them often. We should (all of us) have a treasury of happy memories to sustain us when life is unbearably cruel, to brighten the gloom a little, to be stars shining through the darkness." Thanks Nate and Liam, I'll carry this memory around with me for a while.

Mount Garfield NH

My First Trip into the Sierra Nevada Mountains

Traveling has been a desire of mine since I can remember. As a child, it consisted of reading and imagining what adventures would take place in these unexplored places. The yearning to see, feel, and touch those places never subsided.

J.R.L Anderson describes this yearning in his book entitled *The Ulysses Factor* (3). In this writing, Anderson offers thoughts centered around the exploring instincts of humans. He presents the posit that humans have a predisposed genetic make-up to explore. This genetic pull, if you will, varies in strength from person to person.

In general, some folks are seemingly unaware of a world outside of themselves. Folks of this nature basically sleep-walk through life. Living in a bubble so to speak. Content with the confines of their known world and lacking any desire to step outside of their comfort zone.

Others are somewhat aware of a world outside of themselves but still reluctant, or not interested, in moving outside of their comfort zone. Yet, reading about other places and admiring pictures of those locations piques their interest.

Still others, need to see these places for themselves. At times, these folks travel to a destination, find a safe place to view the environment from and take in the majesty in front of them. Feeling good about what they just witnessed they return to a place of comfort for food and drink.

The feeling of majesty stays with these folks as long as they continue to verbalize their experience and look at the pictures taken of what they saw. Eventually though, these feelings abate and folks return to the daily grind.

Then there are folks who possess a genetic make-up with a strong *Ulysses Factor (3)*. Folks of this nature are not content with the daily drone of society. They desire to explore. The need to see, feel, touch, embrace, and become self-actualized by these adventures is a yearning that drives humans who fall into this category. This yearning, as explained by Anderson, forms the basis of the exploring instincts of man.

I have come to understand that my yearning to explore is innate. For me, a drive that comes from an internal place. Perhaps fueled by my genetic make-up passed on by ancestor's who braved the wild in search of new worlds. Or, maybe, I'm simply a curious man. Whatever the case might be, I feel at peace with myself when I'm exploring new places.

For many years, my desire to travel and explore was put on the shelf in order for me to tend to a set of expectations that society placed in front of me. Exploration, was restricted to reading National Geographic magazines and longing to become self-actualized by the places shown in the pictures.

My earliest recall of my yearning to explore came as a child. Each year our family would take a journey from our home in Sheldon Springs, VT. to the northern part of Maine and my mother's hometown (Houlton). The drive was long. We would leave at 5am and not arrive in Houlton until 7 or so at night. There were no interstate highways then and we drove the back roads of America to get there.

Along the way we would drive past mountains. I remember dreaming about being able to climb them someday. Imagining what it would be like to see the world from the top and longing to get out of the car and put my feet on the ground. Yet, we traveled on.

Another time, I recall visiting the local "book-mobile." In that visit, I stumbled upon a book that described America's National Parks and talked about the adventures of John Muir in places like Yosemite and the Sierra Nevada Mountains. I was captivated by his adventures and secretly desired to go there someday to experience my own adventures. Little did I know at the time that getting there would take years to unfold and be a profound experience in the making.

Life took me on a different path. I spent my youth playing team sports and only occasionally finding time to escape into the woods. I started a career, married young, began a family, and pursued education. I got busy being busy and forgot about my childhood dreams.

Travel mostly came through business trips and later with excursions for sporting events played by my kid's and teams that I coached. But eventually, everything changes. Kid's move-on into their own lives, marriages end, and coaching comes to a conclusion.

When these events played themselves out in my life, the universe decided that it was time for me to start a journey of reinvention. That journey began in a cumbersome manner. I was sick and tired of being sick and tired. I dropped an anchor in my life called alcohol. A crutch placed under me along the journey of life and a substance that no longer had value for me. Removing the crutch required me to stand on my own two feet and face life on life's terms. Life came fast and I had no clue what was happening or what to do with myself. For a while, I wandered around rather aimlessly. Somewhat like a wounded beast trying to find a safe place to heal.

That place came as a result of a very kind person coming into my life. Sherry, picked me up and helped me find my direction again. At first, fear put me in a clouded mindset and I fought the help. Eventually, though, the fear eased and I started to move forward. The beginning of the journey was not smooth. Any trip taken without direction will tend to be that way.

Sherry was persistent, she pushed me to find my pace. As she did, I struggled to keep up. We started walking together, I was so out of shape that I could not walk a mile without stopping. Fear was so ingrained in me that I was convinced that bad things would happen. But we pushed ahead. Moving forward with each step my attitude and outlook on life was going through a transition.

This transition helped me regain my confidence and it enabled me to rekindle hidden desires that were put on the shelf many years ago. The yearning to explore and to find adventure resurfaced. Walks became day hikes, day hikes became "overnighters," and "overnighters" would become weekend hikes.

Eventually, my confidence reached a point where I would be able to start working to satisfy my exploring instincts as described by Anderson in his book. This new found confidence resulted in a plan to hike the Long Trail in Vermont. The thought of hiking 275 miles from one end of Vermont to the other was captivating. The process of planning for the hike was exciting. Sherry was all in. Her support was instrumental. She met me each weekend with food resupplies and provided company by hiking with me as well.

Completing the LT was a great accomplishment for me as an individual. It marked a turning point and helped me realize that life is meant to live in the moment. It is incumbent upon each one of us to find our path forward and to embrace those inner desires that help us achieve some level of self-actualization. It also pushed me to take what has been the most favorite trip of my life; a hike in the Sierra Nevada Mountains of California.

This trip was truly a lifetime in the making. All of those childhood dreams and inner desires to experience this place would come to the forefront of my life. Originally, the plan was to hike the High Sierra Trail from Sequoia National Park to Mt. Whitney. We researched the route, worked to understand the logistics, secured the necessary reservations, and made travel arrangements. Close to our departure date, a wild fire started in the area of Sequoia and Kings Canyon, and close to the High Sierra Trail in Sequoia National Park. We monitored the progress of the fire closely and watched it grow over the course of a couple of weeks. All indications were that the fire was being controlled and we proceeded with our plans. We FedEx'd our fully loaded packs to a hotel in Fresno and a week later boarded the plane. We were on our way.

We were in transit for the entire day from Vermont to California and arrived at our hotel destination in Fresno near midnight. Exhausted, we fell asleep. There was some delay in the delivery of our packs by FedEx to our hotel in Fresno. We spent the early morning hours working to get our packs delivered. Fortunately, FedEx was very helpful and a time was set for the arrival of our packs that was prior to our departure time to Sequoia. For some reason, I decided to check the webcam at Sequoia's Lodgepole Campground which was to be our staging location prior to starting the hike in two days. To my shock, there was nothing to see. Smoke from the forest fire was streaming into Sequoia. Panicked, I called the Sequoia Ranger Station. A Ranger by the name of Heidi answered the phone. I asked about the air quality conditions and the state of the forest fire. We were informed that the fire (now called the Rough Fire) had doubled in size over the last few days and was raging out of control (ultimately it grew to be over 150,000 acres in size). While the High Sierra Trail was still open, the ranger advised us that air quality would be poor and the views would be virtually non-existent.

I didn't know what to do. Fears started to take over and self-doubt crept in. I lamented about the misfortune of the situation. The months of planning and the travel from Vermont. I also asked for advice. Heidi asked if I would mind talking to her husband Lee. According to her, Lee had spent his life roaming through the Sierra Nevada and might be able to help us sort out a plan B. I gave her my cell phone number and hung-up. Within minutes, Lee called. Lee was very congenial and inquisitive. He very carefully gauged our desires, level of experience, and knowledge of the Sierra Nevada. With little hesitation, he helped us carve out a plan B.

We would cancel our reservations for travel and lodging from Fresno to Sequoia. Instead, Lee would route us through Yosemite and into Mammoth Lakes. He informed us that a Yosemite Area Rapid Transit System (YARTS) bus left daily from the Fresno Airport which was across the parking lot of the Piccadilly Inn where we were staying. Lee explained that the route would take us to Yosemite where we could transfer to a bus that would travel to Mammoth Lakes. At Mammoth Lakes, Lee explained that we could go the Inyo National Forest Ranger Station in Mammoth to secure a walk-up permit. He further explained that securing a permit was a near certainty. His reassurance eased some anxiety. Lee explained the trail options from Mammoth to Yosemite in great detail. He offered up suggested side trips that would take us by lakes, around head walls, and over mountain passes. It all seemed overwhelming but his knowledge of the area and confidence in the route he suggested sold us on the idea. The next morning, we were off to an unplanned adventure.

As described, the YARTS bus was on-time and we departed from Fresno to Yosemite at 9am sharp. The ride was exciting as the valley turned into hills and the hills into mountains. Soon, we were in the high Sierra, passing through the tunnel, and into Yosemite National Park. The first images of Yosemite were completely breathtaking from the tunnel view location. I found myself overwhelmed and emotional. Wiping tears from my eyes a sense of disbelief set in. A lifetime of hidden dreams was about to come to fruition. We had a few hours in Yosemite that day and walked around the valley in complete joy while taking it all in.

We boarded the bus to Mammoth Lakes around 4pm. The route ran through Tuolumne Meadows and over Tioga Pass. Stunning vistas came our way around each corner and our excitement continued to grow. We had been able to make a reservation from Fresno for a hotel in Mammoth. We checked in around 8pm and retired soon after.

The next morning, we were up early, ate a solid breakfast, and walked to the Inyo Ranger station. We got there early enough to be near the front of the line. The Ranger was very helpful. We explained our situation and our plan B. The Ranger listened and was very kind by offering suggestions on entry points and with the process of securing our permit. We asked about maps and the Ranger suggested that we purchase a specific one. Within a couple of hours, we were on our way to Reds Meadow to begin our unplanned journey from Mammoth Lakes to Yosemite.

I recall being filled with trepidation as we headed out into the wilderness. I had spent all of my research time becoming familiar with a portion of the Sierra Nevada a few hundred miles away. The trail from Mammoth to Yosemite was a complete unknown. My fear of the unknown and the uncertainty of what we were about to encounter made me very nervous. That nervousness made me edgy and somewhat agitated. Sherry proved to be a great hiking partner once again as she sensed my angst and was patient with me while I worked through my anxiety.

We found a great spot the first night to camp. Like many sites in the Sierra Nevada, it was serene. The setting in the lodgepole pines next to a mountain tarn and surrounded by granite mountains was beautiful. As if by design, a few mule deer wandered into camp. As my tension eased my heart opened up. I began to feel the beauty of this place and accepted the fact that we would get through this journey. A more relaxed mindset was needed and the ability to stay in the moment was a must.

As we journeyed each day, the joy of being in the Sierra Nevada was taking hold. Gratitude for being able to realize a lifelong dream was helping me embrace the joy of each moment. The intense majesty of the entirety of the Sierra Nevada is an awesome experience to have. I was finding deep emotions well up from my reservoir of subconscious thought. Many aspects of the hike are very memorable. But the most memorable time came near the end of our 2-week trek after camping at upper Cathedral Lake.

Sherry presented the thought of climbing up the mountain across the lake. This mountain, called Tressider, looked reasonable so I agreed. Without any idea of what we would find, we climbed up into the granite bowl. A couple hours later, we were near the top of the ridge. We were able to find a route that got us to the top and found a large sandy bench tucked into the side of the ridge and surrounded by Krummholz type trees. It was a perfect place to set-up a tent. Once camp was arranged, we decided to explore. Hopping up to the rim of the ridge line, we were totally astonished. Straight ahead, and 20 miles away, was Yosemite Valley. As we gazed at the beauty in front of us, we embraced views of Clouds

Rest and Half Dome that few people get to see. Yet again, a tear welled in my eye. It's difficult to explain the sense of completeness that permeated through the many layers of my existence and settled in my soul. I can only say that it was a connection to something much bigger than myself, divine in nature, and I embraced the moments with complete reverence of the spiritual event that was unfolding within me.

Many will not understand what I just described. In fact, I'm not completely sure what was taking place in those moments myself. But it was very profound and life changing. This reverence lasted throughout the rest of the day which culminated with watching the sunset in the most serene setting that I have ever experienced.

The next day we explored the area around Tressider in the back-country of Yosemite National Park. I felt fully alive and energized by the spirit of this place. Climbing up and around a unique rock formation called Columbia Finger had me channeling my inner John Muir. I recall that I started thinking about the little boy from Sheldon Springs who stood in awe of this legendary soul and his story of exploring a place of awesome beauty called Yosemite. Having had many dreams about seeing this magical place, feeling the granite mountains, and embracing the majesty here made this an extremely compelling life event. It was as if some sort of connection was unfolding inside of me from a deep and mysterious aspect of my being. The realization and fulfillment of a lifelong dream became a reality, and with it, an opportunity to find a deeper meaning to life.

The unfolding of the events described above was monumental and life altering. By the grace of some power greater than me, I have experienced similar moments, at various times, since then. However, the impact of that awakening in my life has been incredibly fulfilling. It has enabled me to become more open to the divine connection that flows through each soul that walks on earth. I stop short when asked to describe what that divine connection is but have complete faith that it exists. I walked away from that trip with a new outlook on life. Realizing that each day is a gift and meant to be experienced with gratitude.

If I am to take a greater trip in the future, then I look forward to that journey. But for now; my first trip to the Sierra Nevada tops the list.

Tressider Mountain-Yosemite National Park CA

A Presence in the Mountains

One of the greatest benefits of spending time in wilderness settings is the necessity to be present. In some places, where grizzly bears exist, being "bear aware" tends to usher in a connection with each moment. It's all rather primal I suppose. For obvious reasons, the last thing that you want to do is surprise a grizzly bear, or, be surprised by one. Thus, you keep it simple, let go of the distractions, and make sure that you employ all your senses as you make your way. That increased awareness just might help you stay alive.

As you stay present, stillness finds you. With your foot off the mental gas pedal racing thoughts slow down. A gentle hush settles inside, it brings joy and appreciation. I can't discover this treasure if I'm all wrapped up in my own recycling bin of subconscious banter. Therefore, in these natural settings, a slow dissolve takes place.

It doesn't happen all the time for me. The fact is, I'm still living in my human condition which is wrought with inconsistencies. Thus, the slow dissolve comes and goes. Seemingly at the mercy of my own busy brain. But when I pull back from all the striving and soak in the beauty of my surroundings it appears. My own walls come down. Then, an unhurried grace and a tranquil pace find their way in.

One such occurrence happened one August morning in the Teton mountains. While enjoying a cup of coffee on Death Canyon Shelf, that peaceful Presence came. In the stillness of the morning, a misty fog brought in the slow creep of serenity, and it settled within. The early rays of sun streaked across the landscape bringing on a recital of life. It stirred both the flora and the fauna. It also soothed me. In moments like this, you can hear your own heartbeat, feel blood course through your veins, and welcome the rhythm of your breath as the essential element of life.

These moments are quite special, and although infrequent, they happen enough to help raise my awareness. They also leave a lasting impression of what's possible when we fully pass through the veil of distractions that run rampant in everyday life. On this day, within the mystery of a landscape carved over millions of years, the mental and spiritual pollution of our human society faded away.

The frivolous pitfalls of our "modern" times diminished. The mounds of societies waste, the phony smiles of an insincere culture, the empty laughter from soulless places, the greed, the insecurities, the obtuse banality of our civil discourse, the angst, the unrest, and the trappings of addiction. The apps, the ads, the handheld devices of distraction that consume our time and spirit, nowhere to be found. Like the mist of the morning, it all drifted away into oblivion.

As always, the last distractions to leave are the workings of my own mind. Petty thoughts, needless worries, fears, and self-centered obsessions cloud the connection. Ultimately, they too collect into the swirl of the Ego's vortex and quietly flush away. That little squeaking sound from my monkey mind of thoughts becomes completely silent. Even my own desire to scribble down some meaningful words disappears. All of it slowly gone into the arms of the earth by nature's warm embrace. (4)

It took me eight months to get my arms around the deeper stillness that enveloped that morning on the shelf. Sometimes, I'm slow to understand that an ancient perennial philosophy flows through it all and that it is full of Grace. This gift exists within each one of us and it's always available to anyone who chooses to pay attention. Call it what you will, but don't move away from it, move toward it. When you do a kinship is established and all the trivial things in life lose their significance. Instead, a warm gratitude rests within. It brings appreciation for life and the interconnected love that holds it all together. The only gift that keeps on giving and one that brings a deeper meaning to life.

Death Canyon Shelf - Grand Teton National Park WY

Thoughts from the Teton Crest Trail

For 21 years of my life, I had the good fortune of coaching at the University of Vermont for the Men's Ice Hockey team. At the NCAA Division 1 level, I served as the Volunteer Assistant Coach in charge of goaltending development. Aside from a few other assorted tasks, my primary responsibility was to work directly with each athlete to improve their skills as a goaltender. This work required clear communication and collaboration between the coaching staff, the goaltenders, and myself. The more we worked together the better the results. In times when differences got in the way, the less affective we became. As in life, there was no perfection. However, there was perseverance and a collective willingness to endure the tough stretches. There were also many occurrences when our efforts manifested into a high level of performance. At times, even greatness.

Those periods of excellence would not have occurred without a consistent effort by all of those involved. What that effort required is the willingness and internal fortitude to apply oneself to be their best at being better. Put in a simpler context; excellence requires hard work. It doesn't come for free. Being resilient and digging deep to find inner strength when the going gets tough is a valuable lesson to learn. The rewards of learning those lessons are realized continually when they manifest themselves into a life of intention, passion, and purpose. Perhaps even, a mysterious order is stirred that enables the human mind to forget itself for a stretch and to put the Ego on the shelf. For anyone capable of doing that, the universe ensues to heighten your focus and elevate your concentration into a Zen-like place. From that place, consistent performance becomes a possibility that enhances the experience of everyone involved. To this day, those magical moments in time are remembered and shared with those that you journeyed with. Not in a braggadocious way. Instead, it's with a sincere and knowing smile that comes from the memories that you created together. The realization that you faced challenges, uncertainty, and vulnerability (individually and as a group). Then, you overcame it and excelled. Truly, moments of humility and wonder.

With a similar wonder, I take those lessons with me into the mountains. Time in wilderness settings (like Grand Teton National Park) reveal a little more of that mysterious order. The landscape there tends to cradle the heart with awe-inspiring beauty. Towering peaks pierce the heavens, their glaciated slopes, a testament to nature's majesty. Emerald lakes reflect the sky's expanse, capturing moments of serenity in their glassy embrace. The air is crisp with the scent of pine, carrying whispers of ancient forests that shelter diverse wildlife. Thundering waterfalls cascade down rocky cliffs, their energy palpable and humbling. These mountainous landscapes stir the soul, invoking a sense of wonder that transcends mere words. It's a sanctuary where one can't help but feel a profound connection to the Earth's splendor and bear witness to God's Grace. With that Grace comes a measure of humility which brings a source of gratitude. Tranquil seeds of serenity are then planted in your soul. There they take root and nurture growth. The Teton backcountry was a special location that afforded me with the opportunity to pursue a long-time dream. I am better when the Grace of the mountains has a chance to work its magic within my soul. My hiking partners on this trek (Mike and Nate) were both excellent companions and their cooperative friendship enhanced the mountain experience. Much respect and appreciation!

I wish each one of you the very best. We live in an incredibly wonderful place that is full of great people. If you're so inclined, take a few moments as you're reading this message to pause and reflect on the blessings in your life. There are many. Perhaps even take an additional moment to look at the beauty that rests quietly all around us. If you do you might just experience joy and inner peace. May you reflect on these insights with gratitude in your heart!

Throughout our history, many folks espoused the benefits of walking in nature. One in particular, Saint Augustine, once said, "It will be solved in the walking." I tend to agree with that insight. Yet most of the time I'm not always sure what it is that needs to be solved. Therein lies the mystery.

Like John Muir, I find that the mountains lend a cure and offer an opportunity for some introspective thoughts. If I can get out of the way, then I have a chance to learn a little bit more about myself. Sometimes it happens quickly. But most often, it's a slow and gradual process. Regardless, like the roots of trees that work their way into the cracks of rocks to establish a strong foot hold, those meaningful insights can work their way within me and become anchored. Then, without me even realizing it, my awareness increases and new perspectives are formed. The whole process is beyond me, but I appreciate and accept it as a necessary part of my well-being.

As we made our way along the beginning of the Teton Crest Trail, we stopped often to let the surroundings of the area soak in and to absorb the jaw dropping beauty. It was everywhere and it came in the form of a compelling landscape combined with the majestic appearance of large mammals. After spending the previous ten days exploring Yellowstone National Park, you start to feel the immensity of the roughly twenty-two million acres that comprise the Greater Yellowstone Ecosystem (GYE). When you shoulder your backpack and spend a few days walking through a piece of this wilderness it brings the vast expanse of this glorious location home. The realization that this spectacular area of the world has existed for millennia and is constantly under the threat of human impact. Mine included. I owe a debt of gratitude to the countless individuals who have worked to conserve this magnificent location. Those include the Native cultures who lived here for a few thousand years and still call this place home. Then through a complex series of events, and for the last one hundred and fifty years, the National Parks System. Through it all, and the difficult struggles that have ensued, lasting conservation efforts have been led by Native land stewards, experienced wildlife biologists, and passionate journalists who have devoted a large portion of their life to ensuring that the GYE is preserved for future generations. This effort is ongoing and regularly impacted by the politics of greed. As I walked the trail, I held this contrasting reality in my mind. Grateful for the ongoing efforts to preserve these wild places and aware that the challenges of human impact are a powerful force to be reckoned with. For the sake of our collective grandchildren, my hope is that the political forces are held at bay. Our National Parks are sacred for reasons that are more important than money. In a manner that transcends the mind of a venture capitalist, wildlife and these wild places are sacred. They are connected to the soul and must be protected.

With an appreciative mindset at work, we journeyed on. Some notable highlights of the first two days of our hike included the presence of Moose browsing in the distance, a Grizzly Bear ambling along a ridgeline some three hundred yards away, and a stop at Marion Lake for some rest, conversation, and solitude. We also had the good fortune of having a visit with Isaac (from the National Wildlife Federation) who was out taking a survey of Big Horn Sheep. A young man in his late 20's, he was bright, knowledgeable, and engaging. I enjoyed listening to him talk about his work and his backcountry experiences. I also was struck by how easily real conversations readily occur in the wilderness when all of societies apprehensions are left behind. A deep sense of sincerity comes through in an honest and respectful way. As we continued with our walk, we enjoyed a quiet and relaxing lunch at Fox Creek Pass (just below Pass Lake) before finding our way up to Death Canyon Shelf. With a suggestion from Isaac, we stopped at a well-protected camping location with a nearby and reliable water source. Thankfully, we were able to set up our tents, filter water, eat dinner, and safely retreat to our humble shelters as a thunderstorm moved in.

In the mountains, the booms are louder and the flashes of lightening more intense. Somehow though, the experience makes you feel fully alive. After a late afternoon thunderstorm the previous day, came strong winds followed by a steady rain throughout the night. Fortunately, my trusty Big Agnes tent withstood the challenge and I rested well snuggled in my Z-packs sleeping bag. While I remained comfortable and dry on the inside, the rain fly of my tent was quite wet. Thus, as I awoke on my 64th birthday, my first order of business was to hang my rain fly in a tree to dry out a bit. Then, I was able to focus my vision on the beautiful morning that was playing out before me.

Although I try to explain in words, expressing the depth of a mountain experience in writing always seems to come up short. I can offer a perspective and provide a description but I can't bring the elements that touch you through your senses into prose. If you have experienced the sensation of the effects that the elements have on oneself, then perhaps you can relate. Otherwise, perhaps you can imagine. Regardless, the reason that I enjoy prolonged stays in the backcountry is so that I can become uncomfortable. For me it's not a mission to plant a flag on a summit or pound my chest in achievement. I hike and climb to embrace the challenges, experience the sensations, enjoy the air, absorb the views, firsthand, raw, and real. This process of hiking and climbing helps me see the world from a unique perspective. One where I am small and insignificant. Through the mountains, I become right-sized and humbled. I also appreciate the significance of being present in the moment. Like the mountains, I exist. I can conjure up all kinds of meaningful metaphors to help explain that existence. But at this time in my life, I can simply say that being in the mountains helps me understand my purpose.

What is that purpose? Well, if you wonder or care, it's quite simple. Through these mountain experiences I understand that there are many things bigger than myself. Especially the universal guiding force of Grace that is cradled within a Perennial Philosophy. I don't get caught up in slicing and dicing that Grace into a narrative that sounds good. I simply accept it. That Grace offers wisdom and direction. It helps me grow up; psychologically, emotionally, and spiritually. Only then am I able to be of service to others.

To some, the mountains have no meaning. To me, they are meaningful. As I ring with life, so do the mountains ring. That shared vibration brings insight, relevance, and understanding to anyone who allows themselves to listen. I have an appreciation for this truth not in my mind, but in my heart. Only then is the gateway to the soul opened to allow space for the seeds of growth to germinate and prosper. I understand how meaningless it is to try to capture what cannot be expressed in words. Yet, I'm compelled to try.

In quiet solitude my two hiking partners and I let the beauty of the morning work within. We lingered in the glory of the moments and carried that Grace with us over Mount Meek Pass, down the Sheep Steps, and into our side trip up Alaska Basin. There we enjoyed the beauty of a serene setting off the beaten trail. With good fortune on our side, the threatening skies of late afternoon thunderstorms parted and we soaked up the warmth of the evening sun. A glorious way to end my birthday and a gift from above. A very memorable day. I'm grateful for the experience and blessed to be able to embrace these precious moments with good friends.

Hiking off trail brings an opportunity for a deeper level of solitude. Upper Alaska Basin provided us with that experience. The following day would bring excitement, adventure, and a feeling of being at the heart of the Teton Range. As we made our way out of the basin, we met a short but steady climb up to the rise above Sunset Lake. As always in this mountain range, the views were stunning. From the lake came another climb of about 1000 feet to Hurricane Pass. Aptly named, the wind was howling and the depth of the Teton Range spread out directly in front of us. Having held the dream of standing in the center of the Tetons for many years, this moment in time took on a special meaning for me, and it came with heartfelt appreciation. Gratitude ensued.

After a beef stick, cheese, and tortilla lunch, we made our way down the north side of the pass to explore the Schoolroom Glacier and the proglacial lake. Perched on a headwall at roughly 10,400 feet this tiny glacier holds on and its melt water feeds the small lake below. It's also the start of the drainage that forms Cascade Canyon. Over the course of time glacial activity formed the adjacent moraine. Our adventure this day would take us through the remnants of rock, soil, and sediments deposited by retreating glaciers. After exploring the area around the glacier, we headed up and through the moraine in a southeast direction. Having researched and studied the area in advance, route finding was steady and straightforward. Soon we came upon the trail that leads up to Avalanche Divide. We dumped our heavy packs and switched to lightweight day packs that were tucked away in a side pocket of our trail packs. Weighing just a few ounces it was a relief to walk up the trail with the day pack and leave behind the roughly 30lbs of food, water, and gear in our trail packs.

Within a few minutes we reached the divide and were presented with breathtaking views. The immensity of the Grand, Middle, and South Tetons, the depth that makes up the South Fork of Cascade Canyon, the formidable stretch of rock called The Wall, and the incredible wildness and beauty of the upper portions of Avalanche Canyon. With Kit and Snowdrift Lakes below. Each of us stood there without speaking a word. Yet joy was in the air. You could sense it, see it in our eyes, and watch it being expressed from our faces. Truly remarkable moments that were filled with awe. We lingered for a while. Each of us in our own thoughts and absorbing this precious experience in our own personal way. Somehow, we sort of knew what was going on and it was special. As it is in life, and especially in the mountains, these moments don't last forever. But you can choose to let them settle inside and become part of you. I've found that these memories bring a healthy perspective to my existence. I recall them often and the memory always comes with a knowing smile.

With the wind picking up and the cold starting to bite we made our way off the divide, picked up our trail packs, and enjoyed a beautiful walk down to the South Fork of Cascade Canyon to find a campsite and a resting spot for the night. Perched on a rocky ledge just above a brook fed by the Schoolroom Glacier, in a location surrounded by trees, we pitched our tents. Although skies threatened a storm and we got pelted with a few minutes of hail, we averted the storm that poured tons of rain into a canyon north of us. Thankfully, we got to witness the lightening show in the waning sunshine of a great and memorable day in the mountains. As the alpenglow left the sides of the hills I retreated to my tent for the night. Rewinding the events of an epic day in the mountains, and with a heart full of gratitude, I drifted into a peaceful sleep for the night.

We woke the next day to brisk air and bright sunshine. I'll offer some thoughts from a peaceful walk, through Cascade Canyon for your consideration. Too many times I've lived in lost days. Chasing life and forgetting to live. I suppose there is no fault in that way. In some aspects it's called normal. Filled with dualism and the egocentric need to win, to be right, to let the misery fuel the fight. That life certainly brings excitement but it is without substance and hollow to the core. So, we sleepwalk through the days.

As John O'Donohue so eloquently explains in his book *Eternal Echoes* (5), "There is a quiet light that shines in every heart. It calls no attention to itself yet it always shines. Illuminating the way and offering glimpses of beauty, serenity, and peace." The essence of warmth that emanates from this energy brings about possibility, direction, and the awareness of love that sustains a passion for life. It graces our eyes with awe and it enables us to see the wonder that the world reveals to us. Always and everywhere it's there, if only we choose to see. If we do choose to recognize this light then we begin to see the blessings that readily appear in the course of a typical day. Then, nothing ever looks the old way again. By dropping these old ideas one can truly start to live in a world that is full of appreciation, gratitude, and Grace.

Many great books offer insight and paths forward. However, there are no manuals that provide directions on how to construct the individual you would like to become. Only you can decide this and only you can commit to taking up the lifetime of work that it demands. To some the task is too daunting and retreat becomes the driving force. But for those with the fortitude to journey on a wonderful privilege is offered. One that is framed in Grace and warmly presents itself to anyone who is willing to go to any length to find their way through the maze of possibilities that exist. While not always easy, it's an exciting adventure to grow into the person that your deepest longing desires intuitively lead you to be. It is also a great blessing.

With further inspiration from John O'Donohue, finding a creative harmony between one's soul and life is to discover the most precious gift. Certainly, there isn't much that I can do about the great problems of the world. Nor am I able to change the way anyone else chooses to live their life. But by waking up to the eternal beauty and light of my own soul I am better equipped to accept life on life's terms. That acceptance offers me an opportunity to engage in life with a new set of lenses. With that improved vision the internal light of everything glows a little brighter and shines ray of hope. This gift of life is freely given to us for ourselves and also to bring peace, courage, and compassion to others. Thank you, Cascade Canyon, for shining your light.

We had another beautiful campsite for our 5th night on the trail. One that literally had a front porch with a stunning view of Grand Teton. We walked out to an adjoining ledge, a couple hundred feet from camp, to cook our evening dinner and to enjoy the alpenglow on the Grand peak and the walls of North Cascade Canyon as the sun sank into the western horizon. We were joined there by a local guy, named Bryan, who was out roaming around for a few days. Our voices drew him in from his nearby campsite. He was a good guy and we enjoyed an easy conversation about all things in the mountains. One of the simple pleasures of being in the backcountry is that most people leave the angst of society at the trailhead. Thus, the interactions that strangers have tend to be more sincere and respectful. One of the many good lessons to learn from the trail.

As we retired to our tents for the night a peaceful hum resonated through the canyon in a melodic and natural rhythm. It was soothing and relaxing. Peacefully, I drifted off to sleep. A few hours later though I awoke to a strange sound. My initial thoughts were that a jet airplane was flying over the canyon. But the steady roar also came with a high-pitched whistling sound and my mind recalibrated the noise to wind. At first, I detected that the gust must be coming down the South Fork of the canyon from the direction of Hurricane Pass. It seemed logical. But soon the steady and relentless sound was getting louder as it made its way up the north fork. Yet there was no effect of the wind on the canyon floor. Things in my tent and the surrounding trees were still. That calm was about to change.

As quick as the wind gust blew over the canyon walls at some 10,000 feet, it slammed into the headwall above Lake Solitude and circled back low, strong, and steady along the canyon floor. Rattling the trees, shaking my tent, and disrupting the peacefulness of the night. Then, it was gone, or so it seemed. I could hear it echoing from below as it made its way down the canyon. Fading as it went. But not completely silent. In a slow and steady manner, it returned. Repeating the same pattern as before, over and over again. It felt as though the mountains were breathing in their own steady cadence of sleep. I just happened to be there in the heart of the Tetons. Close enough to hear, feel, and experience the natural flow of this majestic range. I felt connected to it all as I fell into my own natural rhythm of sleep in appreciation of the experience.

The next morning was crisp and clear. We made quick work of breaking down camp, packing up, and enjoying our morning coffee with a Pro Bar meal. Fueled for the morning walk we made quick steps to Lake Solitude. Unlike the middle of the day, when throngs of day hikers crowd the area, we were fortunate enough to be the only 3 people at the lake. Quiet, serene, and beautiful, the lake lived up to its name.

Satisfied with our time there, we turned our focus to our climb up the canyon wall to Paintbrush Divide. Slow, steady, and breathtakingly beautiful the trail climbs. I enjoyed every step and was able to maintain a consistent pace up the mountain. In an hour or so I was greeted with strong winds and sunshine at the top. I threw on my beanie and a jacket to fend off the wind gusts. I then set out to explore the area and take in the views. At 10,700 feet the saddle of the divide is uniquely positioned to offer outstanding views in all directions. Though wild, windy, and cold, I enjoyed every second of my time there. Since I departed the lake sooner than my companion's, I was able to capture 20 minutes of solitude in this amazing location. I found a comfortable spot to sit on a recliner styled rock. I used the trail sign and my backpack as windbreakers. They worked well enough to keep me from getting too chilled.

As my mates joined the party, I followed along and enjoyed watching them have their own moments of appreciation for this beautiful place. With the wind gusts increasing we decided to make our way along the knife edged divide. Even though we stayed low and moved steady, the wind tossed us around a bit which made for an exciting moment or two. As we dropped below the ridge line the bulk of the wind was blocked. We made our way down the steep and exposed sections of trail cautiously but without concern.

The walk to Holly Lake offered more breathtaking beauty and the setting around the lake was once again quiet and serene. We enjoyed our last night on the trail in a relaxing and beautiful location. We were greeted by mule deer and welcomed by the resident Picas. A good way to spend our last night in the Teton range.

The last day on the trail always comes with mixed emotions for me. Sort of a combined feeling of Grace, gratitude, and melancholy. For a week, I had the good fortune of being immersed into an environment that I truly enjoy. One that is straightforward, honest, and real. While it might exist there, I have yet to stumble upon anything in nature that comes with pretense. Each element in these natural settings is performing the function that it is intended to perform. I've found this observation to be 100% true with one exception. That anomaly falls into the hands of humans.

I'm not finding fault, mind you. It's simply an observation of myself and my fellow humans. We are a complex bunch. As Alan Watts stated in his book *The Wisdom of Insecurity* (6), "To put it still more plainly: the desire for security and the feeling of insecurity are the same thing. To hold your breath is to lose your breath. A society based on the quest for security is nothing but a breath-retention contest in which everyone is as taut as a drum and as purple as a beet." So, as I made my way out of the backcountry, these thoughts we're playing through my mind.

Having just spent a period of time away from the grind and engaged in a quest, how will I be when I re-enter? "Taut as a drum and as purple as a beet" or will the Grace of nature leave me in a place of perpetual gratitude? In my human condition probably neither and most likely both. Try as I might, I have nothing perfected and I will never reach the lofty place of Nirvana, or to put a more westerly twist to it, heavenly bliss. But, I will (and I do) leave with a deeper awareness of what it is that makes me tick. The inescapable truth is that my attitude and outlook on life is the most insightful approach to gauge my level of acceptance and awareness. When I'm on the spiritual beam nothing and no one bothers me. When I'm off the beam, then everything does. A somber reality or a gift of Grace? I suppose, perspective is key.

Thus, I walked out of my journey with a sense of gratitude for the experience. Perhaps the Picas and Marmots detected my state of mind as they whistled their songs? Or maybe, they knew that in my human condition, I might soon forget the lessons learned along the way? But, most likely, they didn't like me in their home and were screaming at me to go away. Although, they did seem to be as taut as a drum and their cheeks might have been a shade of purple. Maybe, at our core, all of us creatures are the same?

Who knows, the concept of a universal source of well-being might have some merit. One thing is for certain; if you don't find that source in nature, then you'll at least be confronted enough by the elements to think about it. In our human condition, the concept of introspective thought could be the last frontier. Happy trails my friends. Enjoy your journey! We live in a beautiful place!

Climbing up to Paintbrush Divide, Grand Teton National Park

Childhood Memories of Sheldon Springs

I was fortunate to grow up in a small rural town (Sheldon Springs, Vermont). I lived on High Street. The street consisted of 6 tiny brown houses built by the Paper Mill prior to WWII. The head of each household worked at the Mill. In fact, that was the case for practically every household in the town. The 6 houses were productive as there were nearly 30 kids on the street. We ran in packs loosely sorted out by age. My pack was about a dozen strong.

We called the woods behind our street "Down-Back." There was a river that ran through the area, a system of trails that folklore said were made by the Abenaki. We had an island on the river that we could access by wading a small stream and a rock complex that we dubbed "Mayflower Rock" because it was covered with mayflowers in the spring. Adjacent to the river there was a large farm field, a sandpit, a swamp, and a small pond. These woods were our playground and it afforded us the luxury of endless hours of play. What we lacked for in material things, we made up for in imagination. That imagination spurred many creative thoughts.

It was not uncommon for us to lug a shovel and our bikes across the field to the sandpit. We would use the shovels to make a track for our bicycles and spend the rest of the day having races around the track. If we got bored with that activity, then there were cabins, forts, or tree houses to make. We made many. Most often, war games would ensure. Pine cones were grenades, sticks were guns, and chunks of moss were bombs. These activities would eventually run their course and boredom would appear once again. When that boredom hit, a new adventure would be thought up by one of the pack members. On one particular occasion, someone had the idea of building a raft at the small pond near the end of the swamp. The pack embraced the idea and a plan of attack was hatched.

We lugged scrap lumber, nails, and tools over fields and through the woods to a small pond. We spent a couple of days building a raft. We worked in teams and patched together a matrix of creations that somehow ended up connected as one unit that seemed like it would float. Excited to launch the raft, we stripped down to our tighty-whities. It took a solid effort to get the raft into the water. We were elated to see that it floated. With reckless abandon, we climbed aboard and shoved off toward the middle of the pond. Cheers followed and the joy of a successful effort filled our spirits. However, the joy was to be short lived.

As we jostled for position, our raft was stressed under the weight of a dozen squirming kids. Soon, a corner of the raft started to dip deeper in the water. We adjusted to the other side in an attempt to steady the craft. Slowly at first, a piece of wood fell off the raft and drifted away. More water creeped over the edges of our once sturdy vessel. Panic set in and our movements became frantic. The once sturdy vessel could take no more. Seemingly at once, it broke into pieces and each one of us went down with the ship.

Fortunately, the pond was shallow. We were able to wade through the muck and got back to shore safely. The only casualties were the raft and our mud stained tighty-whities. Our laughter echoed through the woods as the comedy of the moment settled in. We sat in the sun drying off as we chewed on the ends of grass and recounted the calamity that just unfolded. After a short while, once again, boredom set in and we set-off toward a new adventure. If no adventure seemed right, then we would play whatever sport was in season.

Mostly, it was baseball. We played practically every day in the summer. While we played organized ball, sandlot games, 500, line-ball, wiffle ball, pickle, or toss and catch occupied most of our summertime fun. We started on the lawn across the street beside the woods. Soon a pitcher's mound, home plate, and base paths were worn into the ground. That area sufficed until we were about 10-12 years old. Our skill levels improved, we were getting a little stronger, and we started hitting the houses with batted balls. It was a poke to do that, and if you hit a house, it was an automatic home run. It was all ok until a window got broken. The parents huddled and came down with a moratorium on baseball games. The other games previously mentioned were still ok to play. But we protested the stoppage to our games.

Our protest did not fall on silent ears. A week or so later, the Mill sent up a few men with chainsaws and a bulldozer. Trees started to fall and a plot of land once covered by trees was turned into a ball-field. The entire street pitched in to help. One of the fathers dragged an old mattress spring behind his truck weighted down with milk cans filled with rocks over the area. We raked, pulled roots, shoveled out the high spots, and did our best to make a level playing field. We built a backstop, paced off the base paths, and planted grass seed. Soon, we had a new field that pointed away from the houses. If you hit the woods, it was an automatic homer and it was about a 250-foot poke. It took a year or two, but eventually, we reached it.

The families on that street were "salt of the earth" people. None perfect, but each a loyal friend. We grew-up together (adults and children). We reveled in each other's successes and cried tears when tragedy struck. I look back at these memories very fondly and feel extremely grateful for having the good fortune of growing up as I did.

Hope in America

America, and the world in general, have gone through monumental changes in the last 60 years. We've all heard members of older generations start a story with an eye-roll-prompting, "Back in my day," which is then followed by a seemingly endless list of ways things have changed in the intervening years (generally portrayed with a negative lens).

However, while those tales of walking 10 miles in the snow may be a little stale, there's no denying that life has changed in some seriously significant ways over the last half-century or so. From advances in technology and medicine to seismic paradigm shifts in romance and religion, life is majorly different today than it was back in the 60's. Yet, some elements of life, like racism, division, and anger, remain in a similar place within the dualistic mind of America.

As a society, we have reaped the benefits of the many advances that have come our way. In the process, our world has become smaller. In spite of certain political traits, our economy has become global and we rely on each other more today than at any other time in our world history. With this growth, and the various advances that have come with it, I also feel that we are losing something that is fundamental to our existence and is paramount to our future survival. That is, our humanity.

Despite all of the various ways that we can connect today, our division is becoming wider. More and more, society is heading down an egocentric path that is self-serving and dualistic. Meaning that there has to be a winner and a loser that is defined by a self-centered viewpoint. Seemingly, many folks are oblivious to the detrimental effects that this life approach has on all of us. In my opinion, if we continue to pull apart as a human race, we will hasten our demise.

In my youth, if you needed a hand, a neighbor was always close by to lend one. In return, you did the same thing when the shoe was on the other foot. Manners, like please and thank you, happened as a matter of course. We held doors for each other and exchanged kind greetings. In general, there was trust in God and in each other. Certainly, these actions take place today. But by and large, they are becoming exceptions to the rule. I believe that they are further diminished when divisive actions are taken.

Of course, back then, a healthy buffer existed between each one of us. Without the advent of social media, we had no idea what deep dark thoughts existed within the minds of each other. Up to the minute posts of how we were processing life didn't exist. The only way that you could get an insight into what a neighbor was having for dinner was if you happened to walk by their home when their windows were open and the breeze was just right. Sometimes, if the smell was good, you might knock on the door and they would invite you in for a meal. Times were simpler then. Frankly, I don't think it's healthy for humans to be in contact with each other 24/7.

Social media has become a flame fest of toxic emotions. Sort of like a psychological dumping ground. Where folks pick sides and engage in cyber war against each other. The calamity being that each side is the same and they go at each other hard in a fruitless battle. Meme upon meme is posted in ridiculous attempts to fortify each other's self-centered beliefs.

It baffles me that while we are in an age where unlimited information is at our fingertips, our culture resorts to nitpicking and name calling, instead of collaborating to build bridges over the gaps that keep the sides apart. Imagine the possibilities that exist in a society that uses a little less ego and a little more understanding.

In spite of it all, there is hope. One by one, and little by little, we can become open to other possibilities. A simple litmus test would be to consider your own attitude and approach to life. Are you a source of compassion, patience, understanding, tolerance, respect, kindness, and love? Or, do you bring, division, anger, frustration, intolerance, fear, resentment, and hate? How each of us proceeds in life is a matter of choice. Faith in something bigger than oneself is a reasonable place to start. Improving your knowledge of spiritual elements and the contrasting effect of a non-spiritual choices is good practice to engage in. The more we know about this aspect of life, the better our chances are of a prosperous future. There is a very good book available called *The Periodic Table of Spiritual Elements*. I encourage you to read it or seek other sources as you desire. Change is needed and it starts with the person that looks back at you from your mirror.

Bravery in an Average Life

T he image of bravery that I have in my brain is one rooted in Hollywood movies. Visions of storming the beach and saving the day dance through my mind. With that image as the backdrop, I can't say that anything that I've done would be considered brave.

To get a better understanding of the definition of bravery I looked up the word in a Merriam-Webster dictionary. Bravery: the quality or state of having or showing mental or moral strength to face danger, fear, or difficulty: the quality or state of being brave. Courage. I can relate to that definition.

In general, I'm just an average guy. I have lived for sixty-something years with no major events coming my way that required heroic measures as defined by Hollywood. However, I have faced elements of danger, fear, and difficulty as I've trudged my road of happy destiny.

Most of these elements have come as a result of having a desire to grow as a person and move outside of comfort zones that I have settled into throughout my life. Stephen King (35) says it well, "The scariest moment is always just before you start."

I have experienced times throughout my life where my desire to move forward was challenged by self-doubt and fear. Most often, the struggle is internal and not apparent to anyone else but me. Working through these times of struggle does take some amount of courage. The fact is, we either face fears, overcome, and grow, or we retreat to a place that we considered safe and known thereby stagnating growth.

In his book, *The Great Divorce*, C.S. Lewis (7) describes that perceived place of safety as our own personal prison cell that we lock from the inside. While the perception of that place is seemingly known and secure, it prevents growth and becomes (in some sense) a living hell. Those brave enough, turn the key, open the door, and move forward into the unknown. At first the going is rough and scary. We struggle and fret over the unknown. Doubt fills our mind and we contemplate turning back many times and at every obstacle. If we can persist a remarkable transformation starts to unfold. As we proceed, we gain confidence in ourselves. What once seemed so daunting and uncomfortable, begins to look like opportunity. As we move forward an attitude of acceptance sets in and a cathartic experience presents itself.

Some say that this catharsis is an example of heaven. Again, Lewis presents a compelling thought about this catharsis, and heaven, in *The Great Divorce* (7, p.69) "That is what mortals misunderstand. They say of some temporal suffering, 'No future bliss can make up for it' not knowing that Heaven, once attained, will work backwards and turn even that agony into a glory." Further: "If we insist on keeping hell (or even earth) we shall not see Heaven: If we accept Heaven, we shall not be able to retain even the smallest and most intimate souvenirs of Hell."

Why then would we ever deny ourselves of that opportunity? As Brene Brown states in her book *Daring Greatly* (8): "we need to cultivate the courage to be uncomfortable and to teach the people around us how to accept discomfort as part of growth."

Being brave enough to muster the courage to face my fears, to go into the wilderness to climb mountains, and to embrace change, has provided me with all kinds of rewards; resulting in a whole new attitude and outlook on life. The result of that new attitude and outlook is gratitude. With gratitude I have a chance each day of enjoying life to its fullest and of being the best version of myself that I can be.

A gift from the divine Grace of the universe.

Thoughts on Wisdom

"As a poet I hold the most archaic values on earth . . . the fertility of the soil, the magic of animals, the power-vision in solitude, the terrifying initiation and rebirth, the love and ecstasy of the dance, the common work of the tribe. I try to hold both history and the wilderness in mind, that my poems may approach the true measure of things and stand against the unbalance and ignorance of our times."
—Gary Snyder (9)

I have known many wise individuals. Men and Women who seemed to have developed a keen insight toward a deep meaning in life. Folks, that were able to sort through the murky ideas and awkward interactions that flow through the normal course of life here on earth. A common theme that has been shared by these wise folks has been a life grounded in an acceptance of who they are as an individual. Not in an overbearing way, but with equanimity, a quiet confidence based in humility, and a belief that they are part of something much bigger than themselves.

Over the course of my life, I have gravitated to people who share the above set of characteristics. Many times, wishing that I had what they had but being too insecure to allow myself to go down a path to find it. As a consequence, lessons taught through my interactions with these folks have been learned slowly over time.

Anthony de Mello states, in his book *Awareness* (10), that "people don't really want to be cured. What they really want is relief, a cure is painful." How true! Curing my insecurities while working on my character flaws and shortcomings was (and is) painful. I mean who wants to take a good hard look at themselves? It's a lot easier to point the finger elsewhere. Thus, when the pain of learning lessons about myself came along, I shied away from them. Yet, life had other plans and those plans continued to bring different people into my life who repeatedly taught the same lessons. Many times, I failed to get the message that the universe was delivering time and again.

Through a series of significant life events, I found myself at a turning point, and in need of a cure. In the serendipitous way that the universe works, I was re-introduced to nature. This re-introduction came rather casually and by way of a walk in the woods. I was pretty beat up and out of shape, so the walk wasn't an easy one. But I found it enjoyable and continued to walk in nature on a regular basis. Soon the mileage would increase and eventually it turned into full-fledged hiking. The more I hiked, the more I enjoyed nature, and the more peace that I found within myself.

Mother Nature and its wisdom was lending me a cure. The Anasazi tribe believes that there is a power in nature that man has ignored and the result has been heartache and pain (11). I find this saying to be true and full of wisdom. From Gary Ferguson's *The Eight Master Lessons of Nature* (12) I got the following story which (with respect to the Ojibwa) I paraphrase for brevity:

> There is also an old Ojibwa legend that talks about a spirit woman giving birth to human twins. As it were, the animal kingdom was left to care for the twins and they found them to be special. The Bear would keep them warm, the Deer would bring them milk, the Birds would sing to them, and the Dogs would chase flies away and dance to make the babies smile. The babies enjoyed the care so well that they stayed in their beds and never learned to walk. So, the wind came and turned stones into butterflies.

Enamored by the beauty of the butterflies, the babies rose from their beds and started to chase the butterflies. And that, say the Ojibwas, is how butterflies taught the children how to walk.

According to the legend, the Ojibwa people tell this story for a reason. They tell the story not to be reminded to not give children everything that they want. They already know that. Instead, they tell the story when people are stuck. When people fall into sadness, or anger, or if they lose hope. The story is told to remind us to first heal our inner relationship with beauty. Inner beauty will help us to start moving again.

Mother Nature helped me to see beauty again at a time when I needed to heal. As a child, I was in the outdoors often. In fact, Down-Back was what we called the woods behind our house. It was a playground and a source of comfort that I embraced. Consequently, nature has always been in me. I wrote the below poem in reflection of a time when nature provided me with a source of comfort as a confused child.

Mayflower Rock Provides Solace...

There is a place down back where the river flows fast
The drone of the mill is muffled

Chaos in the kitchen left behind
Mayflower rock provides solace

The smell of the flowers mixes well
With the muskiness of the moss

A muted sweetness fills the air
Warm breeze touches my face

Sunlight dances through the shadows
Trees sway gently
Leaves rustle a soothing sound
Peace settles in my soul

Prone on the flora
I drift into sleep as the day moves on

Thoughts suspended in a dreamlike state
Senses are dampened

My eyes open to meet the gaze of a deer
Locked in each other's glare

Time slows
Intuitive trust builds

Our connection deepens
Slowly I rise to a sitting position

Uncertainty filters in
The moment is lost

As the deer walks away it pauses
Turning its head our eyes meet again

Affirmation that a connection was made
Evidence of possibilities that exist beyond the chaos in the kitchen

Hope that better things are yet to come
Mayflower rock provides solace

Mother Nature continues to provide me with her wisdom as a man in his sixties. I make a point of paying her a visit often. Sometimes to climb a mountain and sometimes just to sit in solitude and listen to messages that come my way. I find this practice to be extremely enlightening and a refreshing way to live my life. Engaging Nature in this manner has opened a channel of sorts for me and I feel connected to God in ways that I never dreamed of. I wish that I could pass it on to others so that folks would have the same feelings of equanimity that I experience from my time in Nature. But, it's up to each person to find their way. For me, I found my source of wisdom, and each time I visit, I learn a little bit more about myself.

Alone on the mountain...

Alone on the mountain serene is the day
Enjoying the moments passing my way

The din of society left behind
Chirping birds silence the whine

Kerouac's view strange sweet thoughts
Ignorance unkindness fruitlessly wrought

Murky ideas a delusional roll
Angry rants taking a toll

Turn to the source in a quiet place
Embrace the warmth of the Lord's calming grace

Ponder the essence of his wilderness time
A gift for humanity the message sublime

Leconte Canyon, Sierra Nevada Mountains, CA. (Photo by Sherry King)

Lessons From My Parents

At the point of conception, and sprinkled with the divine, gene pools from both sides of the family were combined to produce the essence of life that would become me. After a nine-month period of time, I came into the world and was placed into an environment that would serve as my training ground as I embarked on my journey through life. The primary teachers at the start of this journey were my parents. They cared for me, they nurtured me, and they did their best to lay a solid groundwork of learning that would become the foundation of my education.

In that foundation, my parents instilled within me a set of morals that taught me right from wrong and a value system based in sound life principles such as; honesty, commitment, loyalty, and the necessity of working hard to achieve one's goals. The lessons didn't always come easy for me and the learning environment has not always been idyllic, but there was a consistency of purpose that my parent's brought to the table. Sometimes, my feelings were put in the proper place in a disciplined manner to ensure that the objective behind the lesson was fully understood by me. With respect to morals and values, there was little compromise.

As a strong-minded individual, I didn't always respond well to their approach to parenting. Often times, I was confused by their actions, angry at their methods, and resentful of their approach to discipline. Some of that resentment stayed with me for years. In my developing years, I was not always able to discern why the "spare the rod, spoil the child" approach to life lessons was needed. In retrospect, that approach to parenting was the accepted practice and the established norm for our society during the 1960's. With age and reflection, I can appreciate that my parents had my best interest in mind. There was no selfish motivation in their approach. With my parents' generation; establishing a set of morals and values was their duty as well as their obligation. Anything less would have been unacceptable.

To fully embrace the intent behind the lessons being taught, one should consider the times. My parent's generation has been touted as "the greatest generation" as a result of their perseverance and sacrifices that they made toward freedom during World War II. Because of many great souls from that generation, we are able to experience a life of liberty today.

My father was born in 1925 and my mother in 1933. Ironically, both were born on Christmas day and were raised in a family that consisted of 12 children. They were also born into a developing world that was still reeling from the first World War. As the world stressed to gain its footing, the great depression hit. The impacts of that economic set-back reached far and wide. Luxuries, that we take for granted today, did not exist for my parents. In many ways, folks of that generation lead a hardscrabble life.

In my father's case; he worked at local farms in his youth, often times before school, to bring home eggs or chickens for the family to eat. My mother's family owned a small farm, as a normal aspect of life, she worked to help feed the family. In their recall of these times, neither one of them harbored any resentment toward anyone about their upbringing. Hard work was not only expected, it was accepted as normal, everyone did it. When my father was in high school, World War II was in full swing. His graduation present was enlistment into the Army and a stint in the Pacific War at places like Iwo Jima. My dad never spoke much about his experiences, only to say that we all did what we had to do.

This no-nonsense approach to life was well ingrained into my parents by the time I came along in 1958. With an understanding and appreciation of their backgrounds, I have been able to comprehend why and how the lessons that they imparted on me were important to them. I have also been able to see a bigger picture with respect to how each one of them approached teaching those lessons. There is no doubt in my mind that they loved me and did all that they could for me. I am very grateful for their love, dedication, and devotion to each other, as well as, their entire family. I can't imagine where I would be in my life without the life lessons that my parents imparted on me. Most of these lessons came through their actions.

My dad was a pragmatic person. He was also smart and after WWII attended and graduated from Burlington Business College (later to become Champlain College). He soon became employed by Atlas Plywood and was sent to Houlton Maine as a superintendent of their milling operations. While in Houlton, he met my mother who happened to live across the street from my Uncle Buster and Aunt Olive. Dad lived with them and Uncle Buster worked at Atlas plywood as well.

According to family lore, my grandmother Cyr refuted my fathers repeated requests to date her daughter Yvonne and tried to steer Dad to one of her older daughters. However, Normie was persistent and eventually he won his hearts pursuit. After a period of dating, courting, and frequent visits to the Cyr home, Dad asked for permission to marry his sweetheart, Yvonne.

Soon after their marriage, Dad was transferred from Houlton Maine and back to his hometown of Richford, VT. Normie and Yvonne settled into life and started to raise a family. Their life was going along well as they pursued the American Dream. But life never flows smoothly and Dad was informed that his employer (Atlas Plywood) was closing up shop in Richford. As I understand it, Dad had chances to move to other locations with his employer but all of these relocation's would have taken them farther west and away from New England. I'm sure that this life disturbance came with a fair amount of trepidation. However, seemingly, my father made the best of it and secured a job at the Missisquoi Paper Mill in Sheldon Springs. He worked there for over 30 years until his retirement in 1986. He also worked other odd jobs along the way to bring in extra income. My mother did the same. They worked hard and did their best for their family. In the process, they stayed true to their core set of morals and values.

Throughout my childhood, adolescence, teen, and early adult years, my parents were always good about making sure that life lessons continued to be drilled home. Each one them, and in their own way, stayed true to a core set of morals and values.

From my father it was clear that you needed to take responsibility for yourself. He used straight-forward statements and metaphors to make his points. If you screwed up, he might say, "Well, if you're going to dance, you gotta pay the fiddlers." Meaning there is a price to pay if you screw up, own it and deal with it. Or if you happen to be complaining about a problem in your life, he'd come out with something like this: "If you put your problems on a table with everyone else's, you're always ok with picking up your own and getting on with your life." Meaning everyone has problems, recognize that fact, take care of your own and don't complain about it. If I didn't like the way that something was going on, he might offer the following: "Ok, I hear ya, what are you going to do about it?" Meaning take responsibility for yourself, stop complaining, and take action. In all of these cases he was making sure that you understood where the accountability needed to be placed and that was with the man in the mirror. There was no room for argument, work through it, and take care of your business.

Be that as it may, my dad was always my biggest fan and his support was steadfast. He worked tirelessly behind the scenes to make sure that we had opportunities to play baseball. Through his efforts and determination, he spearheaded the formation of the Missisquoi Little League as well as junior and senior Babe Ruth Leagues. He rarely missed a game and would drive hundreds of miles to be at a baseball or hockey game to support you. It always meant a great deal to me to see him there and it was a sure sign that he loved me and all of his children who he supported equally as well. Later, and in failing health, he did the same thing for his grandchildren. Truly, an outstanding man who was an amazing role model for many.

My Mom always wore her heart on her sleeve. She was quick to laugh, quick to forgive, quick to put you in your place when you were out of line, but mostly she was quick to love. She was also a very kind and compassionate person. At the core of all of this, was a deep faith in God.

Throughout my life, my mother was an example of altruism. It was not uncommon for us to have visitors at our dinner table. Often times, it was a family in need. She never made any issue out of these guests only to make sure that they were treated like family. She also made sure to look after folks who were going through a tough stretch. Be it an illness, a tragedy, or any other disruptive life event, my mom was there to lend her support. Making dinner rolls, loaves of bread, a hot dish, or tending to a person's care, she was a living example of what it meant to be selfless in consideration of others. She would do her best to bring cheer to sad faces and to shine light in dark places. Without doubt, her actions exemplified love.

As I age more (and slowly, but surely, mature), the lessons that my parents left me take on new meaning. Pieces of the puzzle of life fall into place as I continue along my journey. I can draw correlations between my set of life challenges and those that my parents went through. Reflecting on how they responded to those challenges opens me up to receiving more lessons from them.

Watching my children (and now grandchildren) grow and handle their own lives has been a good training ground for me to apply the many great lessons that Normie and Yvonne passed on through their actions. Not one of us can ever get to a place where we master life, and we will always have some level of imperfection with how we respond to it. But, like my parents, I know that if I work hard, do my absolute best, and utilize the set of morals and values that were passed on to me, then I have a chance of coming close to being the best version of myself that I can be.

I am very grateful for the love of my parents and for the many life lessons that they provided along the way.

"Lovelette Family Photo" credit to Lovelette Family archives

Simple Joy

Periodically, Sherry and I take a little stroll up to one of our favorite local mountain spots. Typically, we enjoy kind interactions with strangers we meet along the way, reflect on some of our past journeys, and laugh at the strong cold wind for helping us feel alive. Mountain air and open vistas provide us with an opportunity to reflect on the simple things in life. As John Muir describes in his book *My First Summer in the Sierra* (13), "Oh, these vast, calm, measureless mountain days, inciting at once to work and rest! Days in whose light everything seems equally divine, opening a thousand windows to show us God. Nevermore, however weary, should one faint by the way who gains the blessings of one mountain day; whatever his fate, long life, short life, stormy or calm, he is rich forever."

Mountains also offer silence. Some places of society on the other hand, seem to celebrate in loud talking and live in a place where silence is feared. A conundrum of sorts. How can we ever make sense of the noise without silence? In quiet contemplation we have an opportunity to live in a sacred place. It's a place where we set aside agendas, preferences, priorities, and prejudices. It presents an opening for us to become more aware of others.

With insight from Gabe Smith (14), In that place it's possible to grow in the capacity to sense that we (I or me) are not at the center of things, that our world is not the only world. In the process of this growth, we begin to move beyond the silence into the deeper waters of listening. That change can be scary. But the fear lasts for only a few small moments. If we hang on long enough, we are ready to enter into a new area of life. At first, it might seem uncomfortable. It's true that uncertainty of the unknown can be unsettling. However, we can advance if we simply keep putting one foot in front of the other.

With that approach comes sure and steady progress. In an unassuming way, we find that our inner dialogue shifts from thinking of our next argument to considering the next question we might ask. When we are ready to listen, our posture is less of, "Let me help you understand my perspective" and more of, "Help me understand your perspective."

With silence we have a chance to practice the pause and increase an awareness of others. Simply by listening with just a sliver of curiosity a pathway of communication is opened. It is not a method to gain more control, authority, or influence. It is a lifestyle to become a better neighbor, colleague, and friend.

Over many miles of walking in the mountains you sort of naturally fall into a cadence of contemplative thought. It's a lot easier to do that when it's quiet. Some might even consider times of walking contemplation a form of prayer or moments of mindfulness. Call it what you will, I welcome these moments as they present me with opportunities to connect with a universal goodness that is available to each and every one of us.

Sometimes, I shake my head in confusion with the state of the world. With all of the beauty that surrounds us, why do we bicker with each other and nitpick over our beloved opinions? An unanswered question to ponder in a future walk.

"Unanswered yet, the prayer your lips have pleaded in agony of heart these many years? Does faith begin to fail, is hope declining, and think you all in vain those falling tears? Say not the Father has not heard your prayer. You shall have your desire, sometime, somewhere!" (Ophelia G. Browning) (15)

After one of our hikes, when the above thoughts surfaced, we stopped at the Burger Barn (in Jeffersonville, VT) for a post hike hamburger. While waiting for our order, I sat at our table listening and observing. There were people with skin tones that covered the spectrum of human shades. Folks with tattoos and Harley's. Some with tee shirts emblazoned with a cause that they support. Others dressed in tie-dyed shirts, and some with dreadlocks. I saw old friends exchanging in healthy, respectful, conversation. Sherry and I enjoyed some of that as well.

In the midst of it all, there I was. A pudgy ole boy in his 60's with a slight tinge of post hike body odor wafting into the air. I was accepted too. In quiet moments between conversation, while enjoying my burger, I felt a deep sense of gratitude. Beyond the drama, chaos, and confusion, that plays itself out in the forum of social media, there is a beautiful world playing itself out and running in parallel.

All we need to do is step away from the fray, sit back in silence once in a while, let the peace of that moment settle in, rub some sleep from our eyes, and be grateful. Maybe that's the response to my unanswered question and a place where joy exists.

Spruce Peak Smugglers Notch VT

The Eagle and The Chickens

"The more we learn about man's natural tendencies, the easier it will be to tell him how to be good, how to be happy, how to be fruitful, how to respect himself, how to love, how to fulfill his highest potentialities…The thing to do seems to be to find out what one is really like inside; deep down, as a member of the human species and as a particular individual." Abraham Maslow (16)

Too often, individuals seek fulfillment from the outside to appease the desires of the EGO self. This search is a complex ritual that takes on many faces and is masked by the illusion of a self-centered existence. Many times, the accumulation of things and the approval of others becomes a lifelong quest. In general (and this is very general) the EGO causes fear-based emotions that can make a person seem arrogant when there is a strong desire to be right and an unquenchable need to look good. At the same time, and if you dig under the covers, there is also an element of insecurity at play as the same individual most often feels completely unworthy and goes to great extremes to hide the deep-rooted emotions of self-doubt. Left unattended to, these complex emotions can lead to a life of drama, chaos, and confusion that can shackle a person and limit personal growth.

Becoming aware of other possibilities then seems a worthy pursuit. Otherwise, any given life can be led without ever coming close to realizing one's full potential. I offer a story to consider from Anthony de Mello's book called *Awareness* (17), "A man found an eagle's egg and put it in a nest of a barnyard hen. The eaglet hatched with the brood of chicks and grew up with them. All his life the eagle did what the barnyard chicks did, thinking he was a barnyard chicken. He scratched the earth for worms and insects. He clucked and cackled. And he would thrash his wings and fly a few feet into the air. Years passed and the eagle grew very old. One day he saw a magnificent bird above him in the cloudless sky. It glided in graceful majesty among the powerful wind currents, with scarcely a beat of its strong golden wings. The old eagle looked up in awe. "Who's that?" he asked. "That's the eagle, the king of the birds," said his neighbor. "He belongs to the sky. We belong to the earth—we're chickens." So, the eagle lived and died a chicken, for that's what he thought he was."

For much of my life, I was like the eaglet hatched into a brood of chicks. Pecking away at the earth while clucking and cackling with the barnyard chicks. I'd like to say that I could tell you when I woke up to see other possibilities, but I really can't pin-point an exact place or time. Frankly, I just fell upward when I started to seek a deeper meaning to the constant grind. In some sense, I was sick and tired of being sick and tired. The same old stuff just wasn't working for me any longer. As a consequence, I put in the effort to do some internal data mining. While I have yet to hit the motherlode, I have made some discoveries along the way that have enriched my life. These discoveries have helped me develop a new attitude and outlook on life. The elements of those discoveries are life approaches that bring deep meaning to my life and are the "things that I can't live without."

Physiologically speaking; I need air to breath, water to drink, food to eat, and a temperate environment to live in. These things allow me to sustain life and fuel my existence. Without them, I would perish. When I don't have these basic needs satisfied, I become preoccupied with making sure that they are taken care of. Like the barnyard chicks, I would be scratching away at the earth to exist.

My personal security needs come next. These life elements are related to my personal safety and those of my family as well. Things like a job, money, savings, and housing, all combine to help increase my sense of self and satisfy basic psychological needs. When life events disrupt this aspect of my existence, I become uncertain, insecure, and feel unprotected. Thus, fulfilling these needs is important. While I can live without them, having these items in place gives me the confidence to believe that I can face minor bumps and bruises along the road of life and still be okay.

As a social being, it's important for me to feel like I belong. Family, friends and intimate connections help me through the ups and downs of life. Being involved in life with a community of folks is a natural part of the human existence. Although I do have to be aware that while relationships are an important part of my happiness, they aren't the end all. If I'm solely relying on other people to make me feel ok, then I am sure to be disappointed as my desires are then too egocentric. Likewise, if I go into isolation, my sense of belonging is impacted and depression or loneliness are sure to follow. Consequently, If I am to be happy and healthy, I need to strike a balance in my relationships and make sure that I am not becoming codependent.

That balance can be further established within my self-esteem. If I have the other elements of life in place then I am able to feel a sense of self-esteem that comes from my personal uniqueness and by being loved and embraced by my family and others within my community of interaction. I suspect that each one of us has a natural desire to feel like we are worthy. With that desire comes a need to have our unique talents and capabilities recognized and appreciated. This desire is a requirement of our EGO self that is useful in developing the psychological freedom required to foster a mindset where creativity and growth can flourish.

Developing a growth mindset centered around becoming the best version of myself that I can be is the ultimate goal. In essence, this element of life is me doing my best to be better. If I am relying on input from others, or trying to become something better through acquiring things, I will always come up short. As Abraham Maslow said (18): "What a man can be, he must be. This need we may call self-actualization...It refers to the desire for self-fulfillment, namely, to the tendency for him to become actualized in what he is potentially. This tendency might be phrased as the desire to become more and more what one is, to become everything that one is capable of becoming."

Developing oneself through the guise of self-actualization is a lifelong journey and by no means one that I have perfected. However, my curiosity has been spurred and my inner flame has been lit. Through some sort of divine calling, a perception of something much greater than myself has been activated. With it comes a sense of awe, wonder, and gratitude about life. Truly an awareness of my existence that has changed my attitude and outlook on what living really means. While I care about people, places, and things, I don't waste much time anymore trying to control anyone or anything. Instead, I accept more and when I find myself in conflict, then I accept again. To accomplish that level of acceptance, I need to consider the fact that when I'm in conflict with some element of life it's a signal that there is a resistance formed within me. The fix then, if you will, is within me and not with whatever it is that I choose to point a finger at.

As I progress on the journey, I find that most of my problems are self-induced because some element of my life is out of balance. If I choose to focus on my EGO's desire to be satisfied, then I am allowing myself to be out of balance and pulled away from an opportunity to grow. How I process any aspect of life, and how I respond to any event, is directly correlated to my peace of mind. Being aware of this humbling reality helps me maintain a growth mindset.

With a growth mindset, my perception of reality is less likely to be clouded with self-centered fears or desires. The lenses that I see life through are truer and provide me with a better ability to detect times when my EGO might be fooling me into believing a selfish motivation. Accepting that I make mistakes allows me to be cognizant of the fact that when I do, I can acknowledge them, clear up any confusion or damage that I may have caused, and then make changes within myself to modify my behavior. As mentioned, I am a work in progress and have nothing perfected.

I have also developed an appreciation for prayer and meditation which helps keep the lenses clean that I see life through. This practice helps me to maintain a fresh view of life where I can see the good in myself, others, and nature, with a sense of purpose. I am best able to realize these truths when I am in a place of solitude with my source of Intention. That source for me is a universal goodness that I call God. Many times, I experience reverence within my soul during these times, and through that Grace I receive clarity of thought. EGO tends to go out the window and whatever situation I'm mulling around in my mind seems to become more settled. Solutions then follow that I probably would not have thought of on my own. That's why I seek solitude and why I like to hike. I find out more about myself when I do.

Sometimes, society can seem like a jungle of activity. Tough to navigate through and fraught with danger. Stepping away keeps me centered in the kinship that we have here on earth. With nature, with each other, with ourselves, and with a power that is much greater than all of us. For eons, humanity has made countless attempts to comprehend the incomprehensible. Any attempt that I make at explaining it, will fall short too. I just have faith that this power exists, that it's available to anyone who seeks it, and that each person holds a unique divinity within their soul. Even people that I don't like very much. If I am to continue to grow as an individual, I need to embrace our common kinship and accept the fact that I am but a small part of a much bigger whole.

Hopefully, you can glean out of this rambling that things are not really all that important to me. Striving to get something more from the world or to acquire the latest material thing is not a mission that interests me. Instead, my ambitions move me toward a path that enables me to develop a better freedom of mind. Despite whatever circumstances have (and will) come my way, it is up to me to learn more about who I am and how I respond to life. Aspiring to acquire things seems like a waste of time to me. I lived that life and part of me died in the process.

Instead, I prefer to continue to connect with nature, develop a better understanding of how human beings process life, determine what improvements I need to make within myself, and then do my best to be of maximum service to others. This awareness, when combined with divine guidance, provides me with equanimity at the mind, body, and soul level. I have come to believe that these are the things that I can't live without.

Sterling Pond VT

Dropping the Impulsive Allure

In a conversation with an old friend, I was asked what I've changed my mind about over the years? My response, everything. I live and learn, and then, I live and learn some more. I am a very curious man and I make learning a priority. That priority requires me to embrace learning more about things and more about myself. Sometimes through books and areas of study, while other times through actions that require hands-on learning. As I engage in life, I try to stay in tune with my Intention, Passion, and Purpose. It's my belief that the essence of my engagement here on earth is to continue to develop each day in an attempt to be the best version of myself that I can be and to do my best to help others. The actions that I take toward that end are important and require me to maintain spiritual progress, keep a healthy perspective, and to be less reactive about how life is unfolding.

In my opinion, much of our culture is divisive and toxic. We get bombarded with a constant stream of negative messaging. In a subliminal way, we get brain warped into thinking that we need to say, do, and act a certain way in order to fit in with the group think that we identify with. As a consequence, and sometimes as a default, people can become codependent and lead a transactional existence.

The byproduct of that life approach puts many folks in a mode of reaction. If I say a certain thing, then I can rely on you to counter with an ego stroking response. Our subconscious mind likes the rush of dopamine that we get when this pleasurable feedback floods in. So, we engage in a back-and-forth ritual of validation that helps us feel accepted. These interactions are important with respect to our personality development but can cause damage when not managed well. Similar to the notes that were passed around when I was in elementary school; we basically ask people if they like us and they respond with a yes or a no. A favorable response leads us down a path of acceptance while unfavorable feedback gives us a target to shoot at. Simply put, we like people who like us and are suspicious about people who don't readily agree with us. The lines of what group we belong to are clearly established, a sense of belonging is developed, and our self-esteem is improved with pleasurable feedback from our group.

This process makes it easy for us to find out who is on our side. It also provides us with a supply of enemies that we can project on. These enemies serve an important function for us humans. We know who to dump on and we get to release much of our psychological baggage upon these "deserving" souls. Through ridicule, finger-pointing, backbiting, gossip, and even war, we engage. Our in-groups are formed and the "us vs them" mentality fuels a sort of toxic shame that folks spread through the airways in various forms. We all get affected in a detrimental way by the darkness of these venomous interactions.

This impulsive labeling has been going on since the earliest times of man. Probably a primal defense mechanism put in place over the eons to help us stay safe. Afterall, back in the day, you wanted to be certain that the stranger you let into the cave wasn't going to kill you or steal your food. Perhaps even then people worried themselves sick about other people as alliances were formed and in-groups were developed. Much of the time in today's world, these human interactions take place within the course of the daily grind. For all intents and purposes, most people don't even notice them because it all seems normal.

Like a dog chasing his tail, folks get wrapped up in the drama, chaos, and confusion of codependent interactions. Trying to change people, places, and things, to fit the narrative of the ego is a losing proposition as the depths of the ego's desires are limitless. If you take a step back, and ponder the character traits at play here, you can see the patterns as they work. In a controlling manner, people insist on helping in ways that don't help but instead serve their own desires. During these interactions you can find yourself saying yes when you really want to say no. These ploys really are self-centered efforts being worked by an individual to make other people see things their way. To comply with these impositions, and to appease another's ego, sometimes folks bend over backwards to avoid hurting one's feelings, and in doing so, they end up hurting themselves. Uncertainty ensues and you can then become afraid to trust your own feelings. The pull to belong and feel accepted is so strong that it can make a person believe lies that are being told to them. Later when they find out the truth, they feel betrayed. Ultimately, the cauldron of unmanaged emotions reaches a boiling point. When they do, the urge to get even and punish the perpetrators (or some other suitable target) becomes an unquenchable thirst. Resentment and anger rise from within while another battle line is drawn. A self-fulfilling prophecy works its way that is a bane to our existence here on earth.

Stepping away from this psychotic cyclone of a codependent transactional existence is an option available to each one of us. It simply requires that you make a decision, or elevate your awareness, about what elements of life you deem to be most important. A darkened pathway full of drama, chaos, and confusion or a lighted pathway full of compassion, gratitude, acceptance, and love? In my case, that decision has been a work in progress inside of me for many years and it has required me to be willing to remain open to learning about viewpoints beyond my own. With new knowledge I have become more aware of options that existed and able to choose which pathway was most important to me. You could look at it like a gradual shift in consciousness that has changed the way that I think. This shift doesn't come from me, it comes through me. With it, comes a light that illuminates my soul and puts me in better alignment with a universal goodness that brings with it a meaningful peace.

Becoming aware of the difference between a life lived inside of the psychotic cyclone of a codependent transactional existence, with one lived in the light of a meaningful peace, presents a person with an opportunity to pause and reflect. For me, those opportunities come when I'm out walking around in nature. I can get away from the clamor generated by the grind of the toxic interactions playing themselves out in our society and I can let the quiet of the woods settle my unrest. The solitude found in these moments serves a purpose of cleansing and opens a gateway to elements of life that are restorative. Eastern philosophies call these moments meditative and enlightening while western philosophies label them as being divine. Whatever you call them, they are a welcomed friend and a necessary part of my personal well-being.

Impactful Childhood Experiences

I'm reticent to offer a list of childhood accomplishments. Instead, I offer some childhood experiences that set the stage for my development as an individual. Along the way, milestones have been achieved and things have been accomplished. But those tangible items are not what's the most important to me. In place of those accomplishments is recognition that there has been an on-going energy in my life that has led me to maintain a growth mindset. That energy has become a source for me that provides Intention in my life and a passion to become the best version of me that I can be. Collectively, that pursuit provides me with purpose.

In the early 60's, kindergarten was not a normal step in the education process. I was fortunate to have had the opportunity to attend Mrs. Schoolcraft's 1st ever kindergarten class in Sheldon Springs, VT, in 1963. There were only four of us in the class which meant that each one of us got a lot of attention. The classroom was in Mrs. Schoolcraft's apartment which was located above Joe's Country Store in the middle of town. On most days, instruction was held in her living room. But on really warm days, she held class on a large screened in porch that doubled as an overhang covering the stairway up to her apartment. During reading time, we got to lounge however we liked so that we were relaxed and in a good mood to listen. In the living room, I liked to sit in a corner of her couch. My spot on the porch was in the corner in a soft chair which was adjacent to a large tree. It was relaxing to listen to the soothing voice of our teacher with the soft sounds of rustling leaves in the background. Reading time was a joy, and for me, those experiences created a kinship of sorts with written words. In fact, one that was so strong that it has fueled a lifetime of learning. I was blessed to have been introduced to reading in such a compelling manner.

Perhaps Mrs. Schoolcraft was ahead of her time in her approach to teaching as she regularly incorporated nature into her lessons. Not only were there lessons that involved the natural world, but there were field trips as well. I remember walks through fields chasing butterflies, walking through wooded areas and embracing the majesty of trees, and trips to a nearby stream where we would explore the local flora and fauna. Those excursions opened doors for me and introduced me to a depth of meaning within nature that has piqued my curiosity throughout my life. Wherever you are Mrs. Schoolcraft, thank you!

As I aged, my focus shifted to sports. Baseball and hockey became my heart's desire. I played as much as I could and practiced with friends pretty much on a daily basis as the seasons allowed. Oftentimes, if no one else was around, I practiced by myself. That might mean that I took a bucket of baseballs and bat, stood at the edge of the hayfield behind the house, tossed balls up in the air with one hand while holding a bat in the other, then quickly readied the bat to hit the ball on its descent. Or, I would take a ball and repeatedly toss it up on the roof. Set myself in a good fielding position and practice catching the ball as it fell off from the roof. To practice throwing as a catcher, I would empty the bucket of baseballs and secure the empty bucket up against the tool shed with rocks and wood. When I was in Little League, I would pace off the distance from home plate to second base which is 99 feet, I would then grab a ball, get into my catcher's crouch, imagine a pitch has been thrown and a runner is stealing second base, and then work on throwing the ball with enough accuracy so that it landed inside the bucket. I continued to practice like this as I transitioned from Little League into Babe Ruth and High School ball. But the distance grew to 127 feet on the bigger field.

The practice helped as I was able to play the game reasonably well. I was fortunate enough to make several teams. In the process I was able to play at a higher level (for the area that I grew up in) and perform okay. Along the way, I was awarded a few individual honors. More importantly though, I was taught how to handle adversity, how to handle success, how to work with others, the importance of a positive attitude, and the merits of establishing a solid work ethic.

Hockey in my area of the world was a developing game in the 60's and early 70's. Organization of youth teams was in its infancy and the NHL was just expanding from the original 6, doubling in size from the mid-60's to early 70's. I listened to games on the radio, watched Hockey Night in Canada on Saturday nights which always featured the Montreal Canadiens. During mid-week, we often watched either the Toronto Maple Leafs or the Boston Bruins. Sometimes the reception was so poor that you couldn't get both audio and visual at the same time. So, we often sacrificed sound for a better picture. As snowy as the picture was, you could make out the game and sometimes see the puck. Tuning in the radio gave us an audio feed to enable the full experience of watching sports on TV to be realized. Those memories are great to recall and helped me develop a love for the game.

A love that started the first time that I stepped on the ice at 5 years old. I remember watching the next-door neighbor (Emery Bouthillier) flooding a patch of lawn as winter's cold started to settle in. I was curious and intrigued. I'm not quite sure how it all happened, but I have some recollection of this neighbor explaining that he was making a skating rink and asking me if I wanted to learn how to skate. I must have said OK because I remember him putting skates on my feet and pushing me around on the ice. I'm not sure how I did but I do remember that it was fun and have visions of older kids zipping around. I wanted to do that too. A seed was planted that day.

From that early initiation, playing hockey and skating became a winter passion. We didn't have youth hockey leagues to participate in, so we either flooded a patch of lawn on cold winter nights, found a frozen over wet spot in a field, or went to a nearby iced covered frog pond to play hockey on. If conditions weren't right, then we played street hockey under the only streetlight on our street. I liked to play goalie. There was something about the challenge of defending the cage that resonated with me. My first recall of the dubious pull came when I was seven. My brothers and some of their friends were playing some shiny hockey on the rink beside the house. I wanted to play but was told I was too small, but that I could be the goalie. Seemed like a reasonable risk to take I suppose. So, armed with a baseball glove, a catcher's mask, and a snow shovel as a goalie stick, I jumped into the net. Well, more like two sticks in the snow marking the goal. But it seemed like a net to me. I recall taking a puck to the knee and crying. It stung quite a bit. One of the kid's skated over, told me to stop crying, and that if I wanted to play then I couldn't be a baby. He also gave me some sage advice. That was to crouch low behind the snow shovel and to use it for protection.

We didn't have an abundance of money laying around so purchasing goalie gear was out of the question. To counter that reality, we got resourceful and used catcher's gear, magazines, and a few layers of clothing to provide some protection. I really enjoyed the challenge of stopping the puck and always paid close attention to how the NHL goalies moved. Sometimes, I would shovel off the frog pond by myself and practice goalie moves alone. I got the idea from watching the Howie Meeker hockey school on CBC on Saturday mornings in the winter. Each session ended with a goalie segment starring Buddy Blom. I attempted to copy his instruction all alone on the frog pond. As I recall, I made a shit load of saves there by myself and won a few Stanley cups in my mind. If you're going to dream, why not dream big?

My dream of the NHL never came to fruition, but my chance to play organized hockey did. That chance didn't come until my sophomore year of high school. I actually tried out that year with no goalie gear. I worked all summer to buy a pair of goalie skates but couldn't afford any other equipment. Didn't even own a stick. I borrowed a helmet and some hockey pants from the Lanoue's (a local hockey family) and tried out without any other equipment. My recall is that I could only participate in skating drills until I had goalie gear. After a couple of practices, I finally got to lace on real goalie pads, and handle a few shots, for the first time in the last practice before I got cut. Then a game with the midgets which was the first time that I ever played in an organized hockey game. Through the good graces of local business men, goalie gear was provided and I was handed equipment at my one practice prior to the first game. It didn't matter to me which team I was on. I just was determined to play hockey on a real team and elated to get a chance to do so. Before that chance, I played goal in pond hockey games in the Springs with a makeshift jumble of gear as protection. Playing in a real game with real goalie gear was a big deal for me. I had played that game 1,000 times in my mind and was pumped to get a chance to play. I was also psyched to find out that the puck hurt a lot less when wearing proper equipment. My confidence soared.

I must have played pretty well in that game. As I was skating off the ice after the post-game handshake, I was met at the door by the Bellows Free Academy (BFA) high school coach, Sam Simmons. Sam was quite the intimidating person to me. He had recently graduated from the University of Vermont and was one of the team's better players there. With his new teaching position at BFA, he was also named head hockey coach. He had a big bushy blond afro and sported a matching mustache which framed his face perfectly behind a pair of horned rimmed glasses. He could also skate like the wind and was seemingly comfortable with dropping "F-Bombs" to accentuate whatever coaching moment he was working to instill into the team. When I saw him at the door, my reflex response was fear. I was sure he was going to ream me out for something that I might have done wrong in the game. With my heart in my throat, I stepped through the door.

As it turned out, my fears were unfounded. Instead of a tongue lashing from this man who intimidated me, I met a person at the door who had a great deal of sincerity in his voice and a look of compassion in his eyes.

Coach Simmons complimented me on the game that I had just played. He let me know that my performance impressed him. He said that he might have made a mistake by cutting me and asked me if I wanted to join the high school team as a second goalie. I was dumbfounded and unsure of what was transpiring. Honestly, I don't really remember how I acted on the outside. I want to say that I tried to play it cool but I simply don't know how I appeared. On the inside, fireworks were going off. I couldn't believe what was happening. Somehow, I said yes and at that moment I was on the high school team.

Although I held my own that year, I had a lot of struggles too. Physically with the game and emotionally with being an insecure teenager who was trying to fit in. Coming from a small town and a hardscrabble environment, I was full of self-doubt. I'm pretty sure that Coach Simmons could sense that and I recall times when he would offer words of encouragement or ask me how I was doing with it all. In the process of that season, I developed a trust in him and the belief that he cared about me as an individual. Through my interaction with Sam, I was left with a feeling of hope. With that hope came inspiration. Although I was not aware of it at the time, a new perspective was planted in my mind that season as well. One that was centered on overcoming adversity, setting goals, applying myself to achieve them, and believing that I deserved success. I was also left with the strong impression that a caring, honest, and sincere coach can make a difference in a person's life.

Much of life is shrouded in mystery. It's not always easy to see how the serendipitous pieces of the puzzle fit together to make up each person's unique experience. Life, like the mystery of a mud puddle, is left to one's own perspective. Within that mystery is the beauty of each season of our life. As John Steinbeck stated (19), "What good is the warmth of summer, without the cold of winter to give it sweetness."

A Winter Walk

Snowflakes fall from the sky this morning
Autumn leaves are gone

Hillsides once dressed in vibrant colors
Now draped in a blanket of white

Singing birds muted
Wild geese absent from the sky

The woods are hushed
A wave of silence echoes in my ears

Winter brings reflective thoughts
Grateful images dance in my mind

Solitude in God's creation
Equanimous moments

Prayerful seeds sow
Grace brings its tranquil way

When we look back at the joy that exists within each change of a season, or in the little moments in life, we just might realize that they aren't little moments at all, but the big moments that matter the most. Recognizing these moments and appreciating their impact in your life, might be the greatest accomplishment of all.

Random Acts of Kindness

I n general, I truly believe that we all do our best. Being human, none of us are flawless and each of us comes with some mixture of darkness as well as light. How do these beliefs tie into a random act of kindness? Let me try to explain.

It's not always clear to me when a random act of kindness occurs. How would I know what the mindset is of the person who has decided to give random kindness? There are endless possible mindsets to consider. An act of kindness from one could simply be a normal way of life for another. I also have to consider what my mindset is like when an act of kindness comes my way. At any given point in time, I could be very open to receiving a kind act, somewhat indifferent to a person's kind action, or totally put off by anyone's attempt to be kind. With that set of premises as possibilities, interpreting when a person gives a random act of kindness is subjective at best, it is also tied in closely with my attitude and outlook on life. As a result, it's fair to say that any act of kindness from me (random or otherwise) would be subjected to the same set of premises.

In my humble opinion, the very best that we can do is to be aware of life principles and how they apply to human interaction. That awareness helps us remain open to receiving and giving random acts of kindness. If we are too wrapped up in our own selfish needs then that awareness goes out the window. The one mission of a selfish mindset is to serve the EGO. The EGO has an insatiable appetite and will never be satisfied. All sorts of emotional fallout come along with a self-centered approach to life. Resentment, fear, envy, jealousy, anger, hate, manipulation, as well as many other forms of drama, chaos, and confusion. Being aware of a universal goodness helps us remain open to life qualities such as compassion, patience, tolerance, understanding, mutual respect, kindness, and love.

It really boils down to how each one of us chooses to position ourselves in this world. Do we feed the darkness or feed the light. To the best of my ability, I make attempts to feed the light, to be open to the universal goodness that comes along with that attempt, and to be an example of that goodness. Sometimes I am on point and sometimes I'm not. As noted, I do my best, but I am not perfect.

Waking up, and becoming aware of a set of spiritual principles that offer life qualities based in love and kindness, has enabled me to embrace a way of life that is focused on being of service to others. I do my best to be kind, randomly, or otherwise.

As a result, this awareness, I have witnessed uncountable acts of random kindness from all kinds of people. Frankly, they happen all the time, we just need to be aware. Being open to giving and receiving this element of love that exist in the universe is really all that it takes. We leave our mark as we go.

Footprints left upon the snow

The waning sun casts a glow
Shedding light upon the snow
The path ahead framed in white
Footprints left bathed in light

Behind a track on icy trails
For each journey there is a tale
Visions form of but a few
The mind's eye creates a static view

What were the thoughts carried inside
From each traveler passing by
Good deeds and words to soothe the soul
Perhaps regrets have taken a toll

Uniquely woven within oneself
Experiences stacked on memories shelf
A common thread that humans share
An axe to grind or cross to bear

As well we have a chance to see
The good in life's eternity
Trudge the path look ahead
Embrace the journey with faith your bread

Mystery lurks within each day
Thy will, direction to lead the way
We leave our mark as we go
Like footprints left upon the snow

Underhill State Park-Mount Mansfield VT

Getting to Know Yourself

I have a blessed life that I am grateful for, all of it. From the wonders of exploring the woods called Down-Back as a child in Sheldon Springs, VT, to each and every step that I take along my journey in life. All of the steps matter, good, bad, or indifferent, they are relevant and I have had to put in the effort to keep putting one foot in front of the other. Nothing too earth shattering, just a statement of fact for each of us who climb the mountains of life.

Along the way, transitions have occurred and are what noted philosopher and psychologist William James commonly referred to as the shifting nature of experience and self. While there is no perfection, each of us go through a shifting of our nature with each experience that we gain. Pondering that assertion brings about revelations. The process of pondering also helps sort out the proverbial "wheat from the chaff" and can lead an individual to a place where value can be recognized.

Recently I sent notes of congratulations to a friend who just concluded a 2-year effort of a mountain related pursuit, the inevitable dialogue ensued. What's next? Reference of more endurance goals to follow came the response. As a goal-oriented person myself, I completely understood. However, it got me thinking about all these pursuits that we engage in as humans. What do they mean and what are they for? In most cases we aren't solving complex issues like world peace, racism, homelessness, or global pandemics. So then, where is the value in these pursuits?

I really can't speak for anyone else in that regard (to each their own) so I tapped into my own reservoir of experience. What lasts for me (and the place where it all settles) are the lessons that I learn about myself. The effort and the attitude that it takes to reach a goal are the most rewarding aspects of any achievement, victory, or conquest. At times I've missed the mark. When I have, it's important to remain cognizant of the fact that no personal gain comes without some sort of failure, pain, or sacrifice. Remembering the bigger picture is paramount. With an awareness of how to respond when the outcome of any event is in the balance enables me to maintain a healthier perspective in the daily grind of life. That perspective, when used productively, brings with it, humility. With humility there is a chance of looking beyond my Ego, to give thanks to the source of creation for good health, and the inner resolve to pursue a personal goal (whatever it might be). Each one of us is born with greatness. Sometimes we lack an awareness of that fundamental truth and get too wrapped up in the din of society as well as the perceived expectations that come with it.

In a place of simplicity and quiet listening, one becomes more aware of the ever-increasing separation from the natural world. Wilderness provides a stable point of reference. From a place of patience, we are offered a retreat from the constant flow of human interaction. One that increasingly becomes a forum where people talk at each other without the personal accountability of listening to understand. With ears open to the quietude in nature, a pathway of compassion is created and new perspectives are born. The beauty of the scenery ushers in a little peace and tranquility. Yet, nature is far from simplistic. It can be harsh. It is the home of plants and animals that live within a complex dependency on each other. This same complexity exists in society as well. With our two ears open and our one mouth closed, nature enables one to enter a portal of quiet listening. If we allow ourselves to go there, wilderness then has much to offer each of us within the realm of creation.

In this place of creation, we are offered a glimpse of our own greatness and provided with an opportunity to remember where we came from. From the mysterious realm of life's beginnings each one of us had to persevere through the race for life. Somehow, throughout that competition from a few million challengers, we won and became the individual that we are. Born into an uncertain world of possibility that comes with our own mountains to climb. We forget, or maybe don't consider, these basic truths. We (you and I) are capable of more than we allow. Somewhere deep within each soul lies a mountain of inner resolve. One that continually pokes us. It reminds us to listen to the voice of inspiration that comes from this cosmic reservoir of purpose that generates soul level passion. This place of Grace will fuel your journey if you allow it to. It will also provide you the supply of courage that you need to pursue your own adventure. That fortitude will give you the strength to literally climb your own highest mountain. In some cases, that mountain might be Mt. Everest. In other cases, your mountain will be unique to you. However, a passionate pursuit will enable you to face the challenge with bravery. By engaging in that pursuit, you initiate an intense journey that will bring you home. Where you will experience a more harmonious relationship with yourself and the world around you. Simply because you believed in your worth and you challenged yourself to develop a more harmonious relationship with your own soul.

What then, are we left with? For some insight I consider the thoughtful spirit of John O'Donohue from his book *ANAM CARA – A Book of Celtic Wisdom*. (22) In this lovely book of soul level friendship, O'Donohue delves into immutable topics that weave through everyone who lives within the human condition. The beauty of this wonderful read is impactful at the soul level and it offers timeless wisdom that has served to enhance my journey. With respect to the adventures of life, choosing to live within a peaceful presence is an option for each one of us. Frankly, that place of stillness is simply a vital element in the tranquil place of the soul. Somehow, a unifying source of Grace quietly works in the shadows there. Stitching together little broken pieces of our life into a warm hidden wholeness. In the quietude of nature, we get to listen to the soft whispers of hope that come from this wonderful reservoir of mystical wisdom. These wisdom-based messages of hope and inspiration flow freely. They can help anyone who listens become better acquainted with who they are at the soul level. Maybe even, for the first time.

Embrace the moments of your journey where the stillness lies. In that stillness we get to know ourselves a little more.

"May your trails be crooked, winding, lonesome, dangerous, leading to the most amazing view. May your mountains rise into and above the clouds." Edward Abbey (21)

Cathedral Peak-Yosemite National Park CA

A Friend on The Trail

In July of 2012, I did a through hike of the Long Trail in Vermont. It was an undertaking that had been a goal of mine since my youth. The day-to-day grind of a 275 mile through hike can be difficult. In the course of the hike, one can expect to ascend approximately 68,000 feet in elevation change and descend roughly the same amount. The trail is challenging both physically and mentally. Along the way, there are countless viewpoints to keep your interests. But much of the time the trail runs under the forest canopy and resembles a green tunnel.

Sometimes the green tunnel can be miles long. The views are restricted to trees, rock formations, ledges, as well as flora and fauna germane to the northeast forest environment that the trail runs through. In its own right, I find this environment enjoyable and embraced it much of the time. As mentioned though, a through hike is a grind that challenges a person physically and mentally. These challenges are exacerbated in unpleasant weather. Being tired and sore always seems to make you feel worse when walking in a cold rain or in hot and humid conditions.

One such day occurred for me as I hiked from Little Rock Pond to Minerva Hinchey shelter. The day started out quite nice as I hiked around the pond and up the mountain to White Rocks. White Rocks Mountain is uniquely forested with a large stand of pine trees that cover the mountain. The usual mix of maple, birch, beech, aspen, spruce, and fir, do not exist. The mountain is also unique due to the rock composition of quartzite that was exposed during the last ice age and litter the mountain in white rocks. Walking up and into the forest around the summit, it feels somewhat mysterious and out of place for a Vermont forest. Adding to the mysterious nature of this location are the numerous cairns placed along the trail by AT and LT hikers over the course of time. Hundreds of these tiny man-made works of art have been created in clumps along the way. Sometimes white cairns are scattered in the dozens, and in a couple of spots, a few dozen or more. Walking into these areas has an energy that is difficult to explain. It's as if the spirit of all the through-hikers who walked the path since the early 1900's mingle and greet each passer-by with their good tidings. As a side note; someone took it upon themselves to knock these cairns down a couple of years ago. I was sad when I heard that this act of vandalism took place and can't help but think that the villains who did this dirty deed are haunted by an angry mob of spirit hikers who clang their trekking poles together, echo grunts and groans that only through-hikers hear, and leave the room with a musky hiker smell. Long live the spirit of white rocks. But I digress...

After leaving White Rocks Mountain I had a jump in my step, I felt the energy and the mystery of this unique place along the trail, but this physical elation was to be short lived. It was very hot that day and extremely humid. The heat and humidity hit me hard as I descended the mountain down into Mad Tom notch and crossed route 140. It was a grueling descent and it left me feeling tired. The feeling of fatigue became worse as I started my climb up Bear Mountain. Like many of the ascents on the LT, it didn't appear to be much on the map, but it was a steep and steady climb. I labored hard to reach the summit of this obscure little 3000-foot mountain and felt exhausted when I got there. I still had about 5 miles to go for the day and I felt physically spent. Somehow, I mustered up the determination to continue to move forward. It was a struggle and my spirits were low.

My legs hurt and were cramping as I trudged ahead. I took frequent breaks under the canopy, and whenever I passed a trickle of water, I soaked my head. Regardless, I felt like the energy had been sucked out of me and that I was running on pure determination. I tried to eat a sweet and salty nut bar but could only choke down half of it. I stuffed the rest of it in a side pocket of my backpack. As it is with a through hike, your options in times like these are limited. You either quit and camp on the spot, or suck it up and move on. With my head down and my spirits low, I moved on.

As I walked, I was ruminating about how I was feeling. Not only was I depleted physically, but my mental strength was eroding as well. Thoughts of quitting the trail where circling around my brain. Negative and self-loathing emotions were fueling the downward spiral. I was reaching a low point in my hike and was beginning to feel defeated.

For some odd reason, I stopped, rubbed a mixture of sweat and tears out my eyes, and looked around. I took a few deep breaths, regained my composure, and refocused my thinking. At first, I simply listened. The trees seemed to be whispering a quiet conversation. By that I mean there was a subtle rustling taking place that you can only hear in a deep forest. The song of a wood thrush sang its merry tune and was complemented by a background chorus of other songbirds. In the heat of the day, it was soothing and very relaxing. I started to look around the forest and could see life in abundance; birds flitting about, bugs munching on leaves, bees buzzing along, and a red eft scooting below my feet. I let the moment sink in and it was very peaceful.

Composed, a feeling of delight started to permeate my soul. The self-loathing that engulfed my mind just a few minutes ago was gone. In its place, a deep sense of gratitude. Right about then, my eye caught some movement to my right. As I looked in that direction, I saw a tiny little mouse. It wasn't in a hurry. Instead, it was hopping from stone to stone and it appeared to be glancing up at me every now and then. Curiously, I watched it move.

Soon it was in front of me about a foot or two away. I expected it to continue along it's chosen path. Instead, it stopped and looked up at me. Two big eyes framed by equally big ears all held up by a tiny little body that was about half the size of my thumb. Our eyes locked. This is going to sound strange; I know. But I felt a connection with this little critter. I sensed no fear or angst from this tiny creature. Instead, I felt a friendship of sorts. Much like you would sense a positive vibe from a human that you might casually pass by on the trail.

The little fellow wouldn't ease his gaze. Slowly, I unzipped the side pocket of my backpack and pulled out my half eaten sweet and salty bar. I broke off a small piece, reached down, and placed it in front of the mouse. It never flinched. To my surprise, the mouse looked at the tasty morsel of food, glanced back up at me as if it was looking for approval, and with a little nod from me, proceeded to munch on my gift to him. It took but seconds for the scraps to be devoured. Once again, I expected the mouse to move along. However, he stayed put and returned his friendly gaze to me. So, I broke off a slightly bigger piece of my bar and gently placed it in front of my new trail friend. This time, the piece I offered him was mostly a chunk of peanut. He picked it up with his two front paws. Worked it around a couple of times, to get it just right I suppose, and devoured his treat.

Once he finished, he looked up at me again, paused momentarily, and hopped a couple of stones away to my left. I was expecting to see him scurry off under the leaves and into the long grass to get along with his day. But as my expectations frequently work, I was caught off-guard. The little fellow stopped, turned around and looked up at me. I really have no idea what was taking place in this strange encounter, but it was uniquely special. Instinctively, I slowly dropped down to one knee all the while staying locked in the gaze of this little mouse. I bent over slightly and whispered to my little friend. I expressed gratitude to him for this peaceful little meeting. I told him that I hoped he enjoyed it as much as I did. For a minute or two we were just there in the middle of the wilderness sharing a serene moment.

Satisfied, I suppose, my little friend turned and hopped away. Must be he had some other business to attend to.

A Little Peace of Mind

I found peace of mind when I assumed the responsibility of finding it. In my particular case, I found that responsibility in nature over many miles of walking in solitude. A freedom of thought comes to one's mind in solitude and when a person gets quiet within themselves. By letting go of worldly attachments, a liberation takes place. As Jack Kerouac wrote while spending time on a mountain top, "I decided that when I would go back to the world down there, I'd try to keep my mind clear in the midst of murky human ideas smoking like factories on the horizon through which I could walk, forward…" (22)

American mystic Thomas Merton said (23): "The logic of worldly success rests on a fallacy: the strange error that our perfection depends on the thoughts and opinions and applause of other men! A weird life it is, indeed, to be living always in somebody else's imagination, as if that were the only place in which one could at last become real!" What a strange concept indeed, and one that rests in the minds of many folks in our dualistic thinking society.

The idea of dualistic thinking is that there is an egocentric good and evil which defines the way to be. That people and things should be categorized according to certain standards as seen by the ego. Generally, these standards are set by some type of arbitrary belief system. With these standards comes an accepted conviction that our side has the better ideas. If you don't agree then you're less than we are and lack purity of thought.

The repercussions of this type of life approach leads to toxic shaming of those who don't comply and is a feeding frenzy of unrest.

Dualistic thinking is the way that most people think and act, it is the "us vs them" mentality that is so prevalent today. It brings to some the internal comfort of knowing that they are part of the self-proclaimed inner circle. The inner circle helps one feel reassured that their thoughts are the correct ones, a person then feels vindicated that they are right, and others are wrong. It also allows for a psychological purging to take place through the practice of projecting. Psychological projection is a defense mechanism in which the human ego defends itself against unconscious impulses or qualities by denying their existence in themselves, while attributing the same set of quirks and idiosyncrasies onto others. For example, a bully may project their own feelings of vulnerability onto a chosen target. Dualistic thinking feeds the ego and perpetuates the flames of fear and judgement (24). As Merton says, a weird life it is.

But, at the same time, dualistic and egocentric thinking is a part of life for each one of us. Lacking an awareness of the tricks that these thought processes bring to our mind, puts us in a mode of reaction. Elements of fear and judgement braid their way into our thought process and create an unsettling vision of the world. With an "us vs them" mentality, how can there ever be any semblance of "peace of mind"? Living in this type of mindset brings with it a state of unrest. Nothing is ever okay because there is always someone or something that doesn't comply with one's own set of wishes. Thus, "peace of mind" becomes an elusive target and one that can only be hit when all the forces of the universe align to appease the EGO self. Quite simply, that isn't going to happen! Dualistic and egocentric thinking will always be messy as there can never be the perfect world that this type of mindset requires.

With insight from Judy Leif *How Not to Freak Out* (25), it's possible to realize that to work toward "peace of mind" one needs to start accepting more and releasing their grip on their attachment to self-centered thinking. The use of the word "work" is a bit of a misnomer. In fact, to enable soul-level personal freedom, one really needs to work less and release more. Taking the action to release your attachments brings about liberation and the fallacy of oversimplification brought on by the very things that you become attached to.

Although our Ego likes to tell us a different story, there isn't a world that's more perfect somewhere else. We only have this one world, and it can be quite disheveled at times. If I allow myself to take the easy way out, then the pathway of dualism seems to make perfect sense. In fact, it feels good because it reinforces one's desire for validation. As mentioned previously, the Ego can never be satisfied. It will always leave us in a messy place.

In his book, *Looking for God in Messy Places*, (26) Jake Owensby offers us keen observations to consider as we journey along through life. The fact is, we all worship something. The question becomes, what value does this worship bring to life? Not just your life, but to those around you as well. Certainly, a valid point to consider. Are my thoughts full of fear, pain, despair, and negativity? Am I privately scheming some sort of disaster recovery plan because of the actions that I'm planning to take? Our thought patterns and the habitual actions that follow reveal the type of worship that we allow to exist within ourselves. If I'm locked into a mindset of inner turmoil, it's a message from the Universe that I'm paying attention to a less productive form of inspiration. Other choices are available that return a more productive result. In his book, *The World's Religions* (27) p. 390, Huston Smith offers some thoughtful discoveries. Wisdom-based lessons are readily available to help one understand various options to consider. Each one of us gets to make our own choice on how we proceed. Listening to understand helps me realize that I need to choose wisely.

I have found meaningful considerations from *Brother David Steindl-Rast the way of silence – Engaging the Sacred in Daily Life*. (28) I found many solid messages of hope and direction in Brother David's thoughtful musings. A few of those stood out as paramount for anyone who decides to take on the responsibility of nurturing their own "peace of mind".

In my human condition I live in a profound paradox. So does everyone else. I'm not unique in that regard. In some sort of poetic expression, the instant I stop thinking about myself is the exact moment that a little peace of mind finds me. This happens in a mystical way, and it brings along a warm kindness, a love if you will. Now there are all kinds of thoughts, theories, and philosophies about what this experience is. If I allow myself to get caught up in defining it all, then I immediately start to think about myself more. When I do that, peace of mind floats away. I then have less of it and I'm back to where I started. Similar, I suppose, to thinking about breathing. Which breath is more important, the in-breath or the out-breath? Try it for yourself. I've discovered that they have equal value. Much like the paradox that's being referenced here. To receive the mindful grace of peace of mind, I need to think less of myself and more of myself at the same time. By losing myself I find myself. And so, it goes.

If I allow myself to accept this truth, which I regularly do, some wonderful experiences come my way that are life altering and fulfilling. As an example, when I walk in nature, I do my best to appreciate the beauty that surrounds me. Just simply being present enough to see that my cadence is in rhythm with my breathing and that I am aware of how my feet are touching the ground. It's important that my eyes are not clouded by visions from a flood of thoughts in my mind. But that they are open to see the beauty that rest before me. I need to let go of the distractions of my busy brain and open my ears to hear the subtle sounds of the forest. The rustle of the leaves, the moans and hums from the trees, the songs of the birds and echoes from the calls of other wildlife. I make attempts to feel life in the moments that I walk. Wind on my face, sunlight on my skin, cold, warmth, moisture in the air, they all bring life in abundance. With that life is a certain smell. One that is unique to the day and the specific set of qualities that make up the moments. It leaves a tangible taste in the air that can only be experienced by being present in the moment. Beauty is abundant and works in its everlasting way.

As life unfolds for me, new perspectives develop and new opportunities to respond occur. In each instance, I get a chance to make choices. That's why it's important for me to have an internal GPS that helps me stay the course and set new directions in my life. With this guidance system in place, I am better able to understand paths that I've traveled and more prepared to select the best route forward as life branches out in different directions while my journey continues.

Similar, in fact, to the way a tree grows. Branches develop, they live and prosper, then they die off as new branches sprout higher up the tree. This living and dying off process is a necessary (and critical) part of the tree's growth. Life for human beings is similar. Like the tree, we grow; physically, mindfully, and spiritually. As we grow, our belief system evolves like branches on a tree. Ideologies are formed, live for a while, then die off as new perspectives are gained. Accepting this natural process fosters a more peaceful existence as we are more inclined to let the river of life flow and embrace the process of growth. For us as individuals, as well as everyone else. Lack of acceptance, on the other hand, puts us in a constant state of conflict.

To help me maintain balance in my life, I try to remain aware of a few simple things that are centered around my Intention, Passion, and Purpose.

1) Intention: to have an aim, a plan, a goal

2) Passion: a strong liking or desire toward a specific objective or goal

3) Purpose: a direction for one to follow, an aim toward a goal

My Intention needs to be calibrated each day. I can waver, cheat the system if you will, and not be honest with myself. Faith in a God of my understanding keeps me focused and sets a clear direction for me to follow. It gives me strength and determination in the moments of my day and enables me to stay on course. Keeping my eye on the prize and helping me draw inspiration from the Universal source of all things. A source that is limitless and available to anyone who seeks alignment with the power of that Grace. It comes to me in simple terms through prayer and meditation.

My Passion is fueled by my Intention. My Faith gives me belief and what I believe I can achieve. With the power of my source of Intention, I am empowered to see the winner within. I know I am worthy and I deserve to be the best version of myself that I can be today "IF" I put in the effort. Nothing in life is free. I get one day and that day is today. It is my gift and it is up to me to make my moments count. Being passionate about my life, and the gifts that I have, provides me with a strong desire to be the best version of me that I can be. It also helps me understand that this is an inside job and it's contingent upon me to keep my side of the street clean.

My Purpose aligns with my Intention and Passion. If I am not connected to my source and fueled by my belief system, then I am a rudderless ship. Moving along at the mercy of the wind and the chaos of the stormy seas. With Intention and Passion, I have my hands on the wheel, the wheel is connected to the rudder, and my system is synchronized toward the objective of my Purpose. To be clear, sometimes the going gets tough, and I might consider packing it in, during those moments, feelings of doubt and fear rear their ugly heads. Having a purpose that is aligned with my Intention and Passion sets a path forward. It gives me direction and a deep-rooted drive to continue to trudge ahead. Like climbing a mountain, there will be moments when I have to face my inner fears and conquer the negative voices of self-doubt. My Purpose helps me narrow my focus, silence the self-defeating din, and gives me an inner resolve to forge ahead. Powering through these moments is the essence of my growth as a human being and keeps me moving forward toward my daily goal of staying aligned with my source of Intention.

To help in the process, it's important for me to have a check and balance system in place. A spiritual litmus test of sorts that helps me stay calibrated and gives me a better chance of being a channel of peace in my daily life. With the aid of a wonderful book by Barry John Johnson (*The Periodic Table of Spiritual Elements – The Alchemy of Awakening*) (29), I was able to compile the following list. This list is a snapshot of important distinctions to make as I go through the moments of my day. This list is like a trail system for me and it helps me navigate through life with a better awareness of options that are available to me each time I make a choice about how I respond to life.

The first word is a spiritual element of life centered in Grace and the 2nd word is a contrasting (or egocentric) element of life.

<u>Compassion vs Judgement:</u>

- Compassion is having concern for others and their wellbeing.

- Judgement or being Judgmental is having an excessively critical point of view about something or someone.

<u>Patience vs Short Sightedness:</u>

- Patience is the capacity to accept or tolerate delay, trouble, or suffering without getting angry or upset.

- Short Sightedness is a self-centered view that does not allow for the consideration of others.

<u>Understanding vs Ignorance:</u>

- Understanding is being sympathetically aware of other people's feelings; tolerant and forgiving.

- Ignorance is lacking a desire to consider another point of view or to expand one's knowledge.

<u>Tolerance vs Contempt:</u>

- Tolerance is allowing, permitting, or having acceptance of an action, idea, object, or person which one dislikes or disagrees with.

- Contempt is a pattern of attitudes and behavior, often toward an individual or group, but sometimes towards an ideology, which has the characteristics of disgust and anger.

Respect vs Self Importance:

- Respect is a positive feeling or action shown towards someone or something considered important, or held in high esteem or regard. It conveys a sense of admiration for good or valuable qualities.

- Self-Importance is an exaggerated sense of one's own value, importance, or opinion.

Kindness vs Cruelty:

- Kindness is a behavior marked by ethical characteristics, a pleasant disposition, and concern and consideration for others. It is considered a virtue, and is recognized as a value in many cultures and spiritual paths.

- Cruelty is the action of inflicting suffering or inaction towards another's suffering when a clear remedy is readily available and feeling a sense of satisfaction through the action of being cruel.

Acceptance vs Resistance:

- Acceptance is a person's assent to the reality of a situation, recognizing a process or condition without attempting to change it or protest it.

- Resistance is the refusal to accept or comply with something; the attempt to prevent something by action, argument, manipulation, or control.

Love vs Hate:

- Love is the embodiment of all spiritual virtues. It does not delight in evil or vengeful ways. It rejoices in the truth, it protects, it hopes, it perseveres with a spirit of appreciation for each individual, for the beauty in nature, and in alignment with the source of Universal Grace (A Higher Power).

- Hate is an emotion that causes animosity, anger, or resentment, which can be used against certain individuals, or ideas. Hatred is often associated with feelings of anger, disgust and a disposition towards the source of hostility. Hate leads toward distrust and evil. It also fuels the self-centered desires of the EGO.

It has been important for me to develop a better awareness of all of the above. Without it, I am a fish out of water. Flopping around and gasping for air in a futile attempt to live. With a better understanding of the above, equanimity is within reach. Equanimity brings with it a state of psychological stability and composure which is undisturbed by experience of or exposure to emotions, pain, or other phenomena that may cause others to lose the balance of their mind (30). With equanimity comes a humility that provides a grounding effect for anyone willing to be open to Grace. Is my Intention, Passion, and Purpose aligned with that Grace, or is it not? A simple but important distinction to make that requires me to be honest with myself. Again, being open to Grace allows me to fall into the flow of life without much of a splash and the choices become more apparent. Am I aligned with Grace or am I not?

That Grace is what brings me "peace of mind." I find it throughout my day, but mostly when I am outside and in nature. Sometimes as I quietly walk along a mountain path, sit at a remote vista, or sense the beauty of the moment that I'm in, a feeling of reverence rests within my soul. I come to the realization that I am a small and insignificant part of a living and breathing organism floating through space. Something that is mysterious, scary, and wonderfully beautiful. The magnitude and meaning of it all is incomprehensible to my feeble humanity. Yet, in those exact moments I also experience a deep sense of gratitude for being where I am and who I am. These moments bring me peace and cause quiet reflection.

They are the times when I am best suited to appreciate the fullness of life that comes from the Grace of my source of Intention. My passions are then realized and the significance of my insignificance is aligned with my purpose. It is the place where my peace of mind exists.

Yoho National Park, British Columbia, Canada

A Paradigm Shift

At some point within the process of my development as a human being, I came to the realization that a lot of people (myself included) lived in a place of fear. Not the kind of primal fear that instinctively causes you to run if you're being chased by a grizzly bear, but a toxic fear that is rooted in self-doubt and shame. It's the kind of fear that can keep you in a box, force you to build walls around yourself, and prevent you from becoming the best version of yourself that you can be. It can create a bunker of dualism where one's desire to protect the ego self also serves to separate the individual from the divine Grace of the soul.

In a splintered state, how can anyone become their best version of themself? There will always be an imbalance that creates a conflict of some sort stemming from the division that lies within. As a result of that inner division, one can find themself living in an underlying state of drama, chaos, and confusion brought on by the power of the ego. Nothing will ever be good enough with an individual that fosters a life approach centered on egocentricity. The net of that life approach is unrest. If you aren't okay with who you are and aligned with the source of your intention, then how can you be okay with any other person, place, or thing?

In an attempt to ease the unrest, our subconscious mind creates a scorecard where we track wins and losses, and with that scorecard, we develop an us vs them attitude that creates a mindset of division. In a natural way then, it becomes important to know who is on our side so that we can feel safe with who we allow into our bunker, and in the process, build our tribe. Afterall, if we have a common enemy, then we can always agree on who to point the finger of blame toward. It seldom (if ever) is ourself and this practice of laying blame serves the desires of the ego and allows individuals to project their angst onto others. As a consequence of this dubious practice, comfort sets in, fear subsides, and confidence grows when we feel that it's safe to focus our attention outward with a good friend who reinforces our behavior. The problem with this life approach though is that it is never synchronized. While moments of bliss occur when the universe conspires to provide shots of mutual validation, ultimately, unrest ensues as the world moves on and these moments of bliss fade into the past. In the world of the ego, nothing will ever be good enough.

We are left then, with that unsettling feeling which comes from an ego based-toxic fear eating away at our soul. In the wake of those feelings of despair comes resentment and anger which further serves to fuel the mind with more fear, self-doubt, shame, and pessimism. Folks try to numb these feelings with all sorts of outside stimulants. Some try to numb their unsettledness with substances like drugs and alcohol. While others numb the unrest with too much spending, too much gossip, too much food, or too much of any other self-serving practice. It doesn't really matter what avenue is pursued as long as there is a diversion and we don't have to deal with the source of our problem, which is ourselves. None of these unproductive practices work though as the vortex of the ego is all consuming and unrest continues to fester inside. In fact, the unrest will never subside until we face our inner truth and the divine within. Only then will the voices of fear, self-doubt, shame, and pessimism be silenced as Grace works its everlasting way.

As mentioned, it occurred to me in my process of development (and really at an early age), that fear can control your life. I could see it working in the lives of others and I could see it working in my life as well. For some odd reason though, I could still hear the soft voice of optimism emanating from within that was sending consistent messages of positivity through the din of the pessimistic messages coming from the world. In a gradual and unassuming way, I made a decision to listen to the soft voice of hope coming from within. That choice has made a big impact in my life.

To be honest, my path has not been exponential. There have been starts and stops, restarts and roadblocks, battles with toxic fear and shame, stretches of self-doubt and despair, and periods where resentment and anger pulled me into a mode of pessimistic thought. There have been times when my mettle has been tested and the rays of hope have been dimmed. But, somewhere inside, the soft voice of divine optimism persisted and it kept encouraging me to get up, dust myself off, and try again. Each time that I listened to this Good Orderly Direction (G.O.D.) the volume increased, the message became clearer, and the direction toward doing the next right thing became more concise.

Lack of awareness tends to mute that inner voice and limits our connection. In the words of Aldous Huxley: "The spiritual journey does not consist in arriving at a new destination where a person gains what he did not have, or becomes what he is not. It consists in the dissipation of one's own ignorance concerning one's self and life, and the gradual growth of that understanding which begins the spiritual awakening. The finding of God is a coming to one's self." (31) It took me a while to come to terms with this reality.

For too many years, I chased the proverbial "pot-of-gold" at the end of the rainbow. But the prize seemed like it was always just out of reach. Try as I might, I missed the mark. The more I forced my way to success, the less success I achieved. In essence, the desires of my ego could not be satisfied. I was never good enough, and consequently, it was never good enough. I was a rudderless ship moving along at the mercy of the seas. Peaceful and calm when the sun was shining and the winds of struggle subsided, and bouncing around in a chaotic state when the storms of life blew in. Frankly, I simply was not aware of another way. I knew what I knew and I did not know what I did not know. While I was convinced that my aim was right, I had no Intention, Passion, or Purpose in my life.

The mission that I was on reminds me of Viktor Frankl's remarkably powerful wisdom (*Man's Search for Meaning*) (32), "Again and again I therefore admonish my students in Europe and America: Don't aim at success—the more you aim at it and make it a target, the more you are going to miss it. For success, like happiness, cannot be pursued; it must ensue, and it only does so as the unintended side effect of one's personal dedication to a cause greater than oneself or as the by-product of one's surrender to a person other than oneself. Happiness must happen, and the same holds for success: you have to let it happen by not caring about it. I want you to listen to what your conscience commands you to do and go on to carry it out to the best of your knowledge. Then you will live to see that in the long-run—in the long-run, I say! - success will follow you precisely because you had forgotten to think about it."

As Frankl points out, we need to loosen our grip on attachments as they are desires of the ego. The moment that we realize this reality, we start to wake-up. An awareness then surfaces that allows us to see the road ahead more clearly. Suddenly, and without much fanfare, our rudderless ship has a captain at the wheel and that captain is not me. In that instance, there is a surrendering of self-will that opens up a door to a universal goodness that exists for each one of us. We then start to become what we are seeking. With this increased awareness comes new knowledge and an epiphany of a power greater than oneself. As I know better, I can be better. My Intention, Passion, and Purpose start to synchronize and begin to work in unison with a universe of attraction and energy that is a source of spiritual wisdom. As Fr. Richard Rohr states (33), "As we grow in wisdom, we realize that everything belongs, and everything can be received. We see that life and death are not opposites. They do not cancel one another out; neither do goodness and badness. There is now room for everything to belong. A radical, almost nonsensical "okay-ness" characterizes mature believers, which is why they are often called "holy fools." We don't have to deny, dismiss, defy, or ignore reality anymore. What is, is gradually okay. What is, is the greatest of teachers. At the bottom of all reality is always a deep goodness, or what Thomas Merton called "a hidden wholeness."

With insight from The Franciscan Seculars, and his book *The Soul's Journey into God* (circa 1259) (34), Saint Bonaventure tells us that the "eyes of our souls" should be opened and enlightened so "to guide our feet in the way of that peace which surpasses all understanding". Words like this can inspire us to take the most fruitful journey of our life with confidence and certainty. If we can muster up the courage to open up the eyes of our own soul and take that inner journey, then we can face life with less fear and put toxic shame in its place. We no longer are at the mercy of a dualistic mind that is driven by egocentric thought. We start to realize then that true nobility isn't about being more right or better than someone else. Instead, it's about being right with yourself and your source of Intention which will lead you to a place where you are becoming better than you used to be.

All of these actions start with small decisions. I try to keep it simple each day. In the morning, as I awake, I ask God for direction in my day and that He makes me a channel of his peace. It's very important for my emotional well-being to help me remember that I am a work in progress and that I am better with His guidance as my source of Intention. This guidance fuels a passion for life that gives me a direction to follow and a purpose to pursue. As the result of His spiritual direction, I am more aware of solid life principles that offer me a route to follow as I make my daily climb further up the mountain of life. To be clear, the going isn't always easy and sometimes there are precarious places that I need to navigate through. Left to chance, I could veer off course and risk cliffing out or falling into the abyss below. An awareness of the route, on the other hand, gives me knowledge that the jagged pieces of rock on the cliff face provide hand holds and foot placements that will keep me safe and allow me to make it through whatever rough stretch of climb that I'm going through at the moment. As in life, the small decisions that I make during those times have a big impact on the outcome.

Here are 12 thoughts to consider and reflections on small decisions that make a difference...

1) I can't change the world but I can make the small decisions that change the man in the mirror. As I do, I accept what I see; warts and all. I am ok just as I am and somewhere within my insignificance lies my significance. I accept that truth.

2) I can't have anyone else's life, so instead, I own mine. At certain times in my past, I didn't own it very well. With a source of Intention in my life, I have been able to make changes within myself by accepting the ownership of my attitude and making the small decisions that matter.

3) I am who I am and I try to be honest about that reality. Each day, I ask for direction to be the best version of me that I can be for that day. The small decisions that I make in that regard are what matter most. Simply put, am I being a channel of peace or am I not? I can't dodge that question and I can't fake that approach to life. Be honest!

4) Give it 100%, anything less and I am cheating it, thinking that I'm giving more only serves my ego. To that end, I have to walk the walk and not just talk the talk. The small decisions that I make either get me closer to the light of God and the source or my Intention or farther away. My actions will tell the story of the small decisions. I need to choose wisely.

5) Let go and Let God. My ego self can dredge up all kinds of unproductive thoughts. I need to recognize them for what they are, refuse from an egocentric mind. As I practice a more mindful approach to life, letting go of these unproductive thoughts releases me from my attachment to them it also fosters a heart of forgiveness, within myself and toward others.

6) Practice self-care. I make it a priority to take care of myself. I abstain from ingesting mind-altering substances and I make prayer and meditation a priority, which is a practice that I actively engage in during walks in nature. In those walks, I sometimes fall into the grace of contemplation and let the reverence of the surroundings settle within. With that grace comes a quiet acceptance of myself and the world that I live in. Making the small decision to take these actions makes a big impact on how I view life.

7) Be of service to humanity. That doesn't mean that I'm a martyr. It means that I try to make a distinction with the small decisions that I make regarding my life approach. While these choices might not change the entire world, they have a positive impact on the way that I live and in how I treat others. So, in the interdependent world that we live in, these distinctions matter. By maintaining an awareness of others, I am better able to practice sound spiritual principles in all aspects of my life. Simply put, am I being a channel of peace or not? I can't dodge that question and I can't fake that approach to life. The small decisions that I make in that regard are what matter most.

8) Always be humble and kind. In the wisdom from various spiritual mystics, we are reminded that we should never take the love that life provides us with for granted. Remember your blessings and be grateful for the grace in your life. There is plenty of it and we forget it too often. By making a small decision to keep this simple life principle in the forefront of our minds, we impact the world in countless ways. We help ourselves; we help another human being who receives our kind act, and we help anyone who happens to be witness to that act of kindness. The ripple effect of that one small decision, based in kindness, is immensely impactful and it brings a fullness to life.

9) Remember those who came before you and pay their generosity forward. None of us get where we are without help from others. Parent's, relatives, teachers, coaches, and mentors. Somewhere along the line, each one of us has been impacted by someone else who made a small decision to reach out in generosity. Don't hoard that act of good fortune. Instead make a decision of your own to help others in a similar way or in whatever manner seems suitable to you. If you are generous in life, life will be generous to you. Take these actions with no expectation. If you expect to be thanked for your action of generosity, then I suggest that you rethink your mindset, put your ego on the shelf, and seek direction from a power greater than yourself. If you still question this approach, see #8 above. All the dots connect.

10) Don't let your fears control your life. As Stephen King said, "the scariest moment is always just before you start" (35). All of the trepidation that leads us into a place of self-doubt is a result of egocentric thinking. It's important to remember that each one of us has an incredible reserve of bravery that lies within us. It comes from an incomprehensible power that fuels the movement of the universe. It has inspired greatness across the entire spectrum of humanity and beyond. Make the decision that it can inspire you as well. I have and it has impacted my life in many positive ways. Take a chance, be vulnerable, be approachable, be teachable, take the first step, start the conversation, listen intending to listen and without thinking of what you will say next. Stepping outside of my comfort zone is where growth has occurred. Like a plant transplanted from a pot to the ground, it will become a bigger and stronger version of itself in a very natural way.

11) Improve my spiritual condition on a daily basis. The fact is, I only have a spiritual condition (not a spiritual cure) and it needs to be maintained on a daily basis. Like a garden needs cultivating and weeding, my spiritual condition needs to be nurtured in a similar manner. I can only take that action if I make a decision to improve my conscious contact with God. Further, I can't improve my conscious contact unless I've already made a decision to establish that contact. So again, little decisions have a big impact on how I live my life. It's pretty easy to see how divided we are in the world today. Friends and family turn on each other because of different opinions. People fall into dualistic thinking and pick sides while engaging in battle with someone, someplace, or something without ever attempting to understand another's point of view. With a sound spiritual practice, I can be more compassionate, tolerant, understanding, kind, respectful, and friendly. I can also bring love. By the Grace of God, I can shine light on dark places, simply by doing my best to be a channel of peace. Not always an easy task when dealing with someone who is driven by the power of their own ego, but a worthy pursuit for my own peace of mind. Without a sound spiritual practice, I become like the mountain climber who has no knowledge of the route, the likelihood of peril becomes a real possibility.

12) Be of service to others. If I'm thinking of myself all the time, then I have no time to think of others. With an awareness of the Grace of God, I can be more accepting of others. Life turns from a what's in it for me attitude to an attitude that embraces the coexisting world that we live in. By making the decision to maintain an awareness of others in my life, I open up another pathway to the divine that spreads throughout humanity and is a binding force. If I practice this approach well, then I have to drop the ego-based fear that fuels the voice of judgement. As Jesus said in Matthew 7:3-5; I can't be a hypocrite and look at the speck of wood in my brother's eye until I take the plank of wood out of my own. In other words, I have my own set of quirks and idiosyncrasies to be concerned about. Deal with them first, that effort should last a lifetime. Meanwhile, stop taking yourself so seriously. If I make a decision to understand that I have opinions but not to fall in love with them, then I'm moving in the right direction. Which is away from my ego and closer to God. When I take those actions, I begin to understand and accept whatever it might be that is going on with other people and the world in general. Accepting others as they are, where they are, for who they are, just as they are, is one of the greatest ways to understand others and of having interactions with the most meaning.

Making small decisions based in faith impacts my life in the most productive manner possible. For me, that is spirituality with feeling. It allows me to be with God without overthinking or over-analyzing. This life approach helps me find my way by the Grace of God. My ego-based desires become less important and my vision becomes clearer. As I practice a life centered in prayer and meditation, I am better able to intuitively handle situations that used to baffle me. As I become less of myself, I allow more of God to surface within. With that presence comes direction. I still get in the way every now and again as my will becomes the focus instead of thy will. But mostly, and because of the small decisions that I've made, I go through my day with a calm mind, a loving heart, and a peaceful soul. I don't own this Grace, it comes through me, not from me. I just do my level best to be open to it.

Psalm 46:10 "Be still and know that I am God," is often used as a centering prayer to quiet a busy mind that is cluttered with fear and emotionally built-up energy. It can help ease the inner tension, relax the mind and body, and it can open up a channel that brings inner peace. A centering prayer from Fr. Richard Rohr (36).

Be Still and Know that I am God

Be Still and Know that I AM

Be Still and Know

Be Still

Be

In the midst of it all making a small decision to just, Be, brings with it an impactful amount of serenity. Sometimes I am touched by that Grace, my hope is that you are touched by it too. With all of my love and respect. Keep the faith...

Bow Lake Banff National Park, Alberta, Canada

Acknowledgements

To all the wisdom teachers; the mystics, the holy men, and the holy women who have gone before us. You continue to mentor us all in your mysterious ways. Thank you! I appreciate the kind reviews, discussions, and suggestions offered by family and friends. In particular; Sherry King, Ken Conklin, Barbara Conklin, Ruth Caggige, Tom Novak, Molly Lovelette, Nancy Zottos, Jane Kiser, Nate Patenaude, Mike Haggerty, David McDonald, Stu King, Sheryl King, and Eric Normand. I appreciate your encouragement and thoughtful insight very much. To Mason, Raeya Rose, and Maisie Jade; thank you for your love and inspiration.

Author Bio

Terry Lovelette was raised in Sheldon Springs, VT. and currently lives in Saint Albans, VT. He loves the rolling hills of the Green Mountain State and holds them dear with a sense of loyalty. He is a graduate of Johnson State College. He is retired from a 44-year career in the semiconductor industry. He spent 21 years as a volunteer Assistant Coach for the University of Vermont's Men's Ice Hockey team. He also enjoyed volunteering his time as a USA Hockey Coaching Director in Vermont, as well as a volunteer coach for various youth sports teams. As a passionate outdoor enthusiast, he enjoys an interconnected relationship with nature. His passion has helped fuel a love for hiking. He has walked over 1,000 miles yearly in the last decade and a half. Included in those journeys are through hikes of the Long Trail, The John Muir Trail, the Teton Crest Trail, and various other pathways in desert and mountainous areas of the US and Canada. He is also the author of *Thoughts from a Walk – Green Mountain Musings*. His writings reflect the inspiration that comes from these journeys in a purposeful way.

References

Poetry and Place
  (1) Rick Kempa *Truths of the Trail*. Deep Wild Press. 2024. P. 109

Lessons of Clarity
  (2) Alfred Wainwright *A Pennine Journey: The Story of a Long Walk in 1938*. https://quotefancy.com/quote/2650158/Alfred-Wainwright-The-precious-moments-of-life-are-too-rare-too-valuable-to-be-forgotten

My First Trip into the Sierra Nevada Mountains
  (3) Anderson, John Richard Lane. *The Ulysses Factor: The Exploring Instinct in Man*, J.R.L. Anderson. New York, Harcourt Brace Jovanovich. 1970.

A Presence in the Mountains
  (4) Lusvardi, Anthony SJ. *Nature is your church – The spirituality the land offers is anything but easy* – Plough. 29 August 2017. https://www.plough.com/en/topics/faith/prayer/nature-is-your-church

Thoughts from The Teton Crest Trail
  (5) John O'Donohue *Eternal Echoes: Celtic Reflections on Our Yearning to Belong*. Harper Collins, 2009, page 102
  (6) Watts, Alan, 1915-1973. 2011. *The Wisdom of Insecurity: A Message for an Age of Anxiety*. New York, Vintage Books, a division of Random House, Inc. Maria Popova, 6 January 2014. https://www.themarginalian.org/2014/01/06/alan-watts-wisdom-of-insecurity-1/

Bravery in an Average Life

(7) Lewis, C.S. 1898-1963. *The Great Divorce*. C.S. Lewis Pte. Ltd. Copyright renewed 1973 C.S. Lewis Pte. Ltd. HarperCollins Publishers. P. 69

(8) Brown, C. Brené. *Daring Greatly*: how the courage to be vulnerable transforms the way we live, love, parent, and lead / Brené Brown. - 1st ed. Gotham Books. P. 163

(35) *On Writing* – Stephen King (West of the Sun, October 4, 2017)

Thoughts on Wisdom

(9) Quote by Gary Snyder. https://www.goodreads.com/quotes/12190-as-a-poet-i-hold-the-most-archaic-values-on

(10) de Mello, Anthony, 1931-1987. *Awareness: The Perils and Opportunities of Reality*. Image. Nick Wignall, 27 March 2022. https://nickwignall.com/return-to-wonder-a-review-of-awareness-by-anthony-de-mello/

(11) Roz Savage, 13 August 2020, *Indigenous Wisdom*. https://www.rozsavage.com/indigenous-wisdom/

(12) Ferguson, Gary, 1956 – Author, *The Eight Master Lessons of Nature – What Nature Teaches Us About Living Well in the World*, Dutton 2019. p. 235

Simple Joy

(13) Muir, John, 1838-1914. *My Fist Summer in the Sierra*, Penguin Books 1997 P. 61

(14) Gabe Smith, 3rd Source.com, https://www.3rdsource.com/insights/listening-its-a-lost-art

(15) XXX, Dr. Carolyn J. Eckert, 27 May 2020, https://reflectionsofaminddweller.com/f/unanswered-yet (In 1879, Ophelia G. Browning wrote the poem, *Unanswered Yet?* It was published in 1880 under the pseudonym F.G. Browning. Charles Tillman placed music to the words and it was published as a hymn in 1883.)

The Eagle and The Chickens

(16) (Mark K. Setton, D.Phil., CEO & Founder) https://www.pur-suit-of-happiness.org/history-of-happiness/abraham-maslow/. (Maslow, 1987, p. 6)

(17) de Mello, Anthony, 1931-1987. *Awareness: The Perils and Opportunities of Reality.* Image. p. 3

(18) (Mark K. Setton, D. Phil., CEO & Founder) https://www.pur-suit-of-happiness.org/history-of-happiness/abraham-maslow/. (Maslow, 1954, Motivation and Personality, p. 93)

Impactful Childhood Experiences

(19) John Steinbeck, *Travels with Charley: In Search of America.* https://www.goodreads.com/quotes/54619-what-good-is-the-warmth-of-summer-without-the-cold

Getting to Know Yourself

(20) O'Donohue, John. *Anam Cara: A Book of Celtic Wisdom.* Harper Perennial 1997. Jo Lawrence-Mills, 11 August 2017 https://www.jolawrencemills.info/blog/2017/8/11/return-to-yourself

(21) Abbey, Edward. *Desert Solitaire.* 1968. The University of Arizona Press. https://www.abbeyweb.net/introduction.html

A Little Peace of Mind

(22) Kerouac, Jack. 1922-1969. *Lonesome Traveler.* 1960. Grove Press. P. 133

(23) Thomas Merton, *Seven Story Mountain.* 1948. Harcourt Brace & Company https://www.goodreads.com/work/quotes/982713-the-seven-storey-mountain

(24) https://en.wikipedia.org/wiki/Psychological_projection

(25) Judy Leif, *Essential Guide Wisdom for Difficult Times: How Not to Freak Out*, p. 7. 2020 Lions Roar Foundation. https://www.lionsroar.com/wp-content/uploads/2024/01/Essential-Guide-Wisdom-for-Difficult-Times.pdf

(26) Owensby, Jake. *Looking for God in Messy Places*. 2021 Abingdon Press. p. 68

(27) Steindl-Rast, Brother David. *The Way of Silence – Engaging The Sacred In Daily Life*. 2016. Franciscan Media. p. 47

(28) Smith, Huston. *The World's Religions*. 1991 HarperCollins. p. 390

(29) Johnson, Barry John. *The Periodic Table of Spiritual Elements – The Alchemy of Awakening*. 2016. Elbow Alchemy Press.

(30) https://en.wikipedia.org/wiki/Equanimity

A Paradigm Shift

(31) https://en.wikipedia.org/wiki/Aldous_Huxley. https://www.goodreads.com/author/quotes/4743887.Andrea_Perron

(32) Viktor Frankl, *Man's Search for Meaning*, 1984, Preface. https://www.goodreads.com/quotes/6871197-again-and-again-i-therefore-admonish-my-students-both-in https://www.thepositiveencourager.global/viktor-frankl-and-his-work-on-meaning/#:~:text=Writing%20in%20the%20preface%20to,are%20going%20to%20miss%20it.

(33) Fr. Richard Rohr. https://cac.org/daily-meditations/growing-into-belonging-and-away-from-the-illusion-of-separation2016-12-01/

(34) https://franciscanseculars.com/the-souls-journey-into-god/

(35) *On Writing* – Stephen King (West of the Sun, October 4 2017) https://medium.com/@westofthesun/on-writing-stephen-king-cd3c054a9020

(36) Fr. Richard Rohr. https://gravitycenter.com/practice/be-still/